# RADICAL BUSINESS

"Read John Davis's new book, *Radical Business*. Why? Because the challenges in today's world are compelling leaders and their companies to determine how they will contribute. Assuming that 'business-as-usual' will work is wrong because data show that people worldwide expect companies to be more positively engaged with society, and that means they must transform. The question is how. John's new book shows what companies and leaders must do to become a collective 'force for good' in a world craving solutions."

–Sharmla Chetty, CEO, Duke Corporate Education

"This is an important book – a tour de force for good. Radical Business is a provocative and inspiring guide to leadership in the 21st century. A time in which the best companies must step up to their responsibility as stewards of social change or risk obsoletion. Yet, at this time of brutal uncertainty, the path to stakeholder value creation is complex and risky. With insights from a career in the front row of leadership, Davis charts a course for those leaders wanting to explore and embrace the challenges facing them. He inspires with examples of leaders who have energized their organizations to live up to their full potential whilst breaking down the formidable task ahead into an achievable framework of ideas, questions, and actions to pursue. This book may be the wake-up call that prompts you to action; it may be part of your organization's risk exploration process or your guide to translating stakeholder insights into transformative solutions. Being a force for good may seem like radical business now but tomorrow, it will simply be business."

–Tremaine du Preez, PhD, Decision Scientist and author of
Decide – The Science and Art of Choosing Wisely and
Raising Thinkers

"John Davis delivers an inspired call to action showing us how business can succeed while also being a force for good. Through his rich use of metaphor and examples from around the world, readers will feel empowered to do the same within their organization. John is a welcomed and needed optimistic voice for the 2020s."
–Michael Netzley, PhD, CEO, Extend My Runway (Singapore)

"At this point in time, organizations are key activation engines for a viable, livable, desirable future. For this to be realized requires a new kind of leadership that draws on 'softer' capabilities – courage, empathy, and dare I say, love. John Davis generously charts a path for this future. One that's grounded, no nonsense, and full of actionable wisdom. The cost is high stakes: you may have to change your mindset and skill up. You may have to question assumptions. It may be uncomfortable or scary. However, failure to change is far higher stakes that can take us all down. This is our moment. Read this book if you lead or seek to lead."
–Renee Lertzman, PhD, Climate psychologist and Founder, Project InsideOut

"As the world appears to continue to spin out of control, Davis' new book offers hope. Taking a values-based approach, the book presents a practical framework for leaders to reassess their organization's contribution to the world, guiding conversations to bring about meaningful, measurable, and substantial change for humanity's biggest problem – ourselves – whilst mobilizing employee engagement, bottom-line impact, and societal good."
–Professor Dr Andrew Sharman, Managing Partner, RMS Switzerland and Chairman of One Percent Safer

"With today's social unrest, unknown economic impacts, and health crisis, it is a challenge for organizations to create societal value. To help companies navigate through this ever-changing environment, John Davis wrote an excellent book, providing

Boards and Executive teams with a guide on how to future-proof their business and realize the company's dream. The book contains practical examples and inspiring insights from various thought leaders. It is empowering. A must read for those companies who do not just want to thrive in today's and future world, but want to drive sustainable change and make an impact."

–Anouk De Blieck, Board Advisor, Non-Executive Director Elliot Scott HR, Senior Industry Advisor WhitewaterTX

"*Radical Business* courageously and justly directs companies to be fit for purpose in an age when we are learning that our long-held assumptions and criteria for success are no longer adequate."

–Adam Kingl, Adjunct Faculty, UCL School of Management and Hult International Business School

**Author of *Next Generation Leadership: How to Ensure Young Talent Will Thrive with Your Organization***

Climate, Biodiversity, and Inequality are some of the severe, connected, and accelerating global crises threatening our dignity and well-being as human beings on this planet.

We must mobilize all available forces for positive change to build the future we all want. We need the contributions from all key partners in society: policymakers, opinion leaders, and the private sector!

Business cannot thrive in societies that fail. Innovation and business development for a better world is probably the most important and most rewarding role of modern companies in the coming decades! Solving environmental and social problems with business models makes sense and makes profits when you get it right.

Business has amazing powers to drive innovation and transformative change! That's good news because we need to change many things to sustain our world. The not so good news is that the business cases of those changes are often unclear, and the complexities of the issues can be overwhelming for business leaders. Both represent barriers for the priorities and actions we need to see in business.

The very good news is that John Davis, with his book *Radical Business*, delivers great help to make business leaders understand, navigate, and succeed in the necessary and rewarding transformation of the role of their companies in society. John provides lots of evidence, examples, insights, and useful tools to help busines leaders rethink their approach to business and organizational development and help to embrace the sustainability challenge as you would embrace any other business opportunity.

The meaningfulness and economic reward from solving environmental and social problems with busines models is huge, today, and even more tomorrow. Business leaders who want to be part of that mission for the benefit of their employees, customers, shareholders, and the world should read *Radical Business* and transform their companies to become more future fit.

Dr. Claus Stig Pedersen Head of Global Sustainability
Novozymes A/S

# RADICAL BUSINESS

How to Transform Your Organization
in the Age of Global Crisis

BY

**JOHN A. DAVIS**
*BrandNewView LLC, USA*

United Kingdom – North America – Japan
India – Malaysia – China

Emerald Publishing Limited
Howard House, Wagon Lane, Bingley BD16 1WA, UK

First edition 2022

**Reprints and permissions service**
Contact: permissions@emeraldinsight.com

**British Library Cataloguing in Publication Data**
A catalogue record for this book is available from the British Library

ISBN: 978-1-80262-808-1 (Print)
ISBN: 978-1-80262-807-4 (Online)
ISBN: 978-1-80262-809-8 (Epub)

ISOQAR certified
Management System,
awarded to Emerald
for adherence to
Environmental
standard
ISO 14001:2004.

Certificate Number 1985
ISO 14001

INVESTOR IN PEOPLE

*To Barb, Kate, Chris, and Bridget. Your love makes anything possible.*

# CONTENTS

# ACKNOWLEDGMENTS

I've had the pleasure to interview hundreds of leaders over the years. Those featured in this book are accomplished, diverse, and inspiring, and I thank each of them for sharing their insights with me. Thank you to: Ravi Kumar, Kate Gordon, Anthony Guerrero, Steve Leonard, Helle Bank Jørgensen, Kevin Czinger, Jonathan Reichental, Rangsiyopash Roongrote, Chip Conley, Mac McKenzie, and Janice Lao. Their examples show that positive change is possible and leads to meaningful impact. Thanks, too, to my Agent, Nick Wallwork of NewsomWallwork, and to Charlotte Maiorana and her team at Emerald Group Publishing.

# INTRODUCTION

*How can a rational being be ennobled by anything that is not obtained by its own exertions?*[1]

—*Mary Wollstonecraft*

In 2001, I was teaching an EMBA class at the University of Washington (UW). For the first 15 years of my career, I had avoided the academic world. I came from an academic family. My dad, both brothers, uncles, aunts, grandparents – most had been academics. I had started a couple of small businesses while in college and those were fun, so I wanted to get better. I was offered jobs in my senior year, including one with Salomon Brothers in New York and the other with Black Angus Restaurants. Salomon paid more the double what Black Angus offered. I took the Black Angus job. As one mentor said to me, the difference isn't the money but the skills. Black Angus would teach me how to run a business. Salomon would teach me how to manipulate spreadsheets. For the next 15 years, including getting my MBA, I worked for startups (my own included), Fortune 500 companies, and in turnarounds. It was exhilarating, but I loathed corporate politics. I gave a talk at UW and the next thing I knew the university invited me to teach. I fell in love with it. The opportunity to teach at Singapore Management University arose and I took it. I started writing and publishing multiple books on business, marketing, and sports. It led to some terrific experiences. I became a full professor of practice; served as department chair at other schools; became Dean at SP Jain School of Global Management; then spent the past few years at Duke CE, heading up Asia from Singapore; and then did the same in the United States. Throughout I worked with leaders of Fortune 1000 companies, learning that many shared a common anxiety: how could they leave their company, and the world, in a better place than they found it. The increasing ferocity of climate crisis storms, social injustice, economic inequality, and global pandemics ushered in an era of extreme vulnerability for humankind. What would it take for businesses everywhere to become a collective force for good, not just makers of goods? That question has nagged at me for years, hence this book.

I am not offering an anodyne set of prescriptions. I am giving you evidence to reinforce that changing how your company does business is possible. Not without cost, of course. But we face a much larger cost if we don't collectively get our act together, do the courageous and right thing, and ensure that our companies start to repair the world, not ravage it further. Businesses have created unrivaled economic prosperity, lifting more people out of extreme poverty, and enlarging middle classes around the world. Important advances and innovations have occurred, often led by the ingenuity of people like you. But as businesses prospered over the past century, invasive extraction of finite resources grew. The precious metals we use in most of our electronics are the by-products of intensive mining practices. Fossil fuels extraction leads to a wide range of petroleum-based by-products, including plastic, which ends up contributing to more than 165 million tons of plastic waste that damages the world's sensitive marine environments.[2] Ocean farming practices help produce our food yet many of those same practices are permanently destroying fish populations. More than a quarter of all-natural medicines have been discovered in the world's tropical forests. Those same forests serve as Earth's lungs, absorbing carbon dioxide and producing oxygen, yet in the past half-century we have destroyed more than one third of all tropical forests and each year over 30,000 square miles of additional deforestation occurs.[3] The impact is clearest with the climate crisis. At the same time, despite the material gains, economic prosperity has been unevenly distributed, worsening wealth disparities and increasing social tensions, and exposing centuries of systemic racism.

This book is a blueprint showing you how to transform your business into a force for social and economic good. The statistics are promising for those companies that invest in innovation, and becoming a force for good will require ingenuity. McKinsey (2020) research shows that when companies invest in innovation during a crisis, they end up outperforming competitors by 10% on market capitalization; and those that invest in innovation post-crisis outperform competitors by 30%.[4] We are in an age where the problems confronting us are unprecedented in scope, scale, and savageness. We need companies from startup to Fortune 100 to innovate, and quickly. Almost any new initiative, product, or venture is fraught with uncertainty. The efforts your company undertakes to transform into a perpetual force for good will test your ability to tolerate failure, stimulate creativity, and be open-minded to people who challenge your every move. I am optimistic. When our backs are against the wall, people have found countless ways to prevail. Yes, businesses fail all the time. But not all fail at the same rate, or the same time, or in the same way. Yet we know that doing nothing will accelerate our path to failure of our global economic, social, and environmental ecosystems. Mixed in with failures are victories and when those are aggregated positive momentum can result. Now is the time for businesses and their leaders everywhere to step up to become a force for social and economic good.

Profits arise from a simple equation: it's the money left over after you have paid all expenses. Over the past few decades, increased profitability has defined business success. Publicly traded companies are rewarded by markets when share prices rise, increasing the value of shares owned. But the focus on profitability limits the potential impact of a company's success to just a narrow group of shareholders, missing a much greater opportunity for the company to positively impact nonshareholder communities. My premise is simple: business leaders today have a wide open door to change their companies for the better by making a deliberate shift away from the profit motive and toward the *societal value motive*, where businesses are a force for good that contributes positively to society, not just makers of goods, strengthening the circular economy (a regenerative economic system that reduces waste and resource demands and keeps the life cycles of products and materials in use for longer). Achieving a circular economy requires companies to update their definition of success.

To reimagine your business's contribution to the world, you must wipe away any pretensions you might have that clever advertising or false claims are the path to redemption. This is not a twentieth century positioning exercise or, even worse, a greenwashing campaign such as Volkswagen engaged in when, in 2015, it was discovered that the automaker had been "using illegal software to conceal poisonous emissions," affecting 11 million diesel vehicles. The damage to VW's reputation was significant, as were the penalties: $39 billion in criminal and civil fines; 6 VW executives were charged; their CEO, Martin Winterkorn, was forced to resigned in disgrace and had to pay VW over $14 million; and one was sentenced to 7 years in prison. And more penalties are expected against the automaker. Why the harsh judgments? An MIT study showed that the excess emissions could lead to 60 deaths in the United States and that 1,200 people in Europe would die prematurely.[5] You can't help but wonder what possible rationale convinced guilty executives that this was a sensible or responsible idea.

While there are no guarantees, there are approaches you can take to improve your chances for creating positive and meaningful impact as you transform your company. You can't change the world alone. Companies need partners for transforming into a force-for-good to work. Those partners include the world's financial markets and regulatory bodies. As you'll see in this book, there are promising signals from BlackRock, TPG, and Norrsken in linking funding to sustainability scorecards. Regulatory bodies like the European Union and the US Securities and Exchange Commission are drafting new green disclosure requirements for companies. Business leaders like Salesforce's Marc Benioff are vocal proponents of companies doing good, and you'll meet several more leaders in this book pushing for change. Tradition-bound thinkers will be formidable opponents. Yet just as some of the most celebrated business leaders have often gone against the grain to put their dent in the universe, today's company leaders must resist conventional business wisdom that focuses on maximizing profits and, instead, think of optimizing social contribution as a new path to financial health.

There is ample evidence that by reimagining a company's contribution to society, financial value will improve. From my research on and work in over 40 countries, I have distilled the principles top performing companies (including startups) demonstrate to create enduring value into 3 main themes and 12 underlying focus areas.

- Section 1 – Value Meaning

- Section 2 – Value Measure

- Section 3 – Value Mobilization

| Section 1 Value Meaning | | Section 2 Value Measure | | Section 3 Value Mobilization | |
|---|---|---|---|---|---|
| Aspiration | Distinction | Reputational | Organizational | Stakeholders | Engagement |
| Culture | Experiences | Societal | Financial | Environment | Solutions |

*Section 1 – Value Meaning* focuses on what your company needs to do to cultivate *meaning* in its work and workplace.

- Chapter 1: Aspiration – *why are we here?*

- Chapter 2: Distinction – *what makes us truly unique?*

- Chapter 3: Culture – *who is involved?*

- Chapter 4: Experiences – *how do we "show up"?*

*Section 2 – Value Measure* focuses on the four dimensions of value that underscore success for top performing organizations.

- Chapter 5: Reputation – *what are we known for?*

- Chapter 6: Organization – *do employees feel like their work matters?*

- Chapter 7: Societal – *are we contributing impactfully to the communities we serve?*

- Chapter 8: Financial – *what factors improve financial value?*

*Section 3 – Value Mobilization* describes the four specific factors required to help get things done.

- Chapter 9: Stakeholders – *what do we really know about them?*

- Chapter 10: Engagement – *how must we captivate those outside our company?*

- Chapter 11: Environment – *how do we ensure our company environments are safe for employees and stakeholders?*

- Chapter 12: Solutions – *how can we create solutions to achieve our aspiration?*

Each of the sections and underlying focus areas are interrelated, and you'll see how your efforts in one impact what you do in another. You're undoubtedly eager so let's get started on radically transforming your business.

## NOTES

1. Wollstonecradt, M. (1792). A vindication of the rights of woman. Chapter 3 (last sentence). Retrieved from https://www.gutenberg.org/cache/epub/3420/pg3420-images.html.
2. Iovino, N. (2020, April 30). Ocean currents found to embed microplastics in seafloor. Courthouse News Service. Retrieved from https://www.courthouse news.com/ocean-currents-found-to-embed-microplastics-in-seafloor/.
3. Deforestation: 11 Facts you need to know. Conservation.org. Retrieved from https://www.conservation.org/stories/11-deforestation-facts-you-need-to-know.
4. Loughlin, R., Jeff, S., Shivam, S., & Scott, W. (2020, October 22). Modern CPG product development calls for a new kind of product manager. McKinsey. Retrieved from https://www.mckinsey.com/business-functions/mckinsey-design/our-insights/modern-cpg-product-development-calls-for-a-new-kind-of-product-manager.
5. Multiple sources: (1) Schwartz, J., & Siebold, S. (2021). Former CW CEO charged with false testimony over diesel scandal. *Reuters*. Retrieved from https://www.reuters.com/business/finance/prosecutors-charge-winterkorn-with-giving-false-testimony-german-parliament-bild-2021-06-09/. (2) Riley, C. (2021, June 9). Volkswagen's ex-CEO pays company $14 million over his role in the diesel scandal. CNN. Retrieved from https://www.cnn.com/2021/06/09/business/volkswagen-martin-winterkorn-dieselgate/index.html. (3) Chu, J. (2017). Study: Volkswagen's excess emissions will lead to 1,200 premature deaths in Europe. *MIT News*. Retrieved from https://news.mit.edu/2017/volkswagen-emissions-premature-deaths-europe-0303.

# Section 1

# VALUE MEANING

# 1

# REIMAGINING ASPIRATION

*Now is the accepted time, not tomorrow, not some more convenient season. It is today that our best work can be done and not some future day or future year.*[1]

–W.E.B. Du Bois

"The world is moving from interconnected to interdependent. Companies are evolving into the town centers of the future and are becoming the platform for driving social changes. You're not safe if your neighbor is not safe. No business will flourish if those around them are not flourishing," says Ravi Kumar, President of Infosys. He believes businesses everywhere have a responsibility to contribute more directly to the vibrancy and success of the communities they serve. Based in New York, Ravi's responsibilities are global. In his 20 years at Infosys, he has seen how digital has made the world more intertwined, the speed at which skills change has also increased, and COVID-19 further accelerated this shift. But many people are behind in these skills, so the company is investing in reskilling and upskilling centers to help people gain the skills needed to succeed in today's technological world and, he believes, it is the right thing to do for society. We are wired to solve problems and with digital tools our ability to do so will be a diminishing virtue since machines will increasingly take on that task. Ravi sees the real opportunity as helping people develop into world-class problem finders, and that means cultivating a person's learnability (the ability to quickly gain understanding and insight).

Higher education in the United States and around the world is at crossroads. Collectively, they still offer students an important education. But most aren't set up to address the skills needed to contribute to today's modern society. Yes, critical thinking and specialization expertise are taught and remain important.

But there is a very large, underserved population that would gain great benefits from the kind of reskilling and upskilling opportunities Infosys is providing. Most elite institutions have seen an extraordinary rise in applications over the past decade, yet most of these schools have not increased their enrollments. While their low admittance rates confer bragging rights for exclusivity, the question remains whether that really serves their institutional purpose and, more broadly, important societal needs. For non-elite universities, such as state university systems, decades of declining state and local tax cuts have eviscerated their budgets, making it harder for them to offer the breadth of subjects and schools for which they were once known and celebrated. Community colleges and polytechnics are impacted as well, with declining budgets reducing the ability to service the needs of people seeking more advanced skills. Education is a vital need common to people everywhere and is part of Infosys' ESG (Environmental, Social, and Governance) efforts aimed at impacting over 80 million lives. There simply aren't enough of the right kind of higher education opportunities for many people, so as Ravi sees it "we're helping to fill that need…" by building an educational infrastructure designed to help people gain the technical prowess they'll need to be impactful contributors to society. Many of the people benefitting from Infosys' educational initiatives may join other organizations. That's fine with Ravi because he sees developing people with digital and technical skills as a societal good. Education is *the* driver to bridge numerous social divides, from social injustice to economic inequality to greater understanding among people everywhere, creating meaningful societal value.[2] Infosys, like many other companies described in this book, is role modeling how businesses everywhere can become a force for good, with its digital and technological education initiatives as a guiding aspiration.

The choices we face to fix today's problems are hard and the solutions may even be contrary to almost everything we've learned about how businesses are supposed to measure success. But ignoring these difficulties won't make today's converging crises disappear, nor will acting in a business-as-usual manner, especially since both are what got us into this massive predicament in the first place. Defining your company's aspiration (its desire to achieve something great) brings to life its purpose (why it is here), setting you on a more successful future path. Havas Media Group (2015) found that companies that *aspired* to improve our quality of life beat the stock market by 120%.[3] Having a clear aspiration improved the chances of transformation success by 300%.[4] Furthermore, business transformation is more successful in companies with a clear purpose according to 84% of executives in a 2020 EY survey, plus they have 30% higher levels of innovation and 40% higher employee retention.[5] From 1996 to 2011, purpose-led companies outperformed the S&P 500 by 10×. Infosys has had a clear purpose for over 40 years: helping companies stay contextually relevant to the times they are in. Upskilling and reskilling is part of the company's belief in developing the talent of the future, stimulating lifelong learning, and is the cornerstone of Ravi's efforts.

Consumer needs are changing significantly worldwide. They are increasingly making purchase decisions based on your company's contribution to society. 53% of South African millennials have walked away from businesses that are not aligned with their values, such as failure to demonstrate concern for the environment.[6] 80% of Gen Z and 85% of millennials in the United States rate a company's reputation for environmental concerns as a primary factor when making purchase decisions, and 79% believe that companies must address social issues.[7-8] 70% of millennials want to work for employers that tackle societal problems. 83% "would be more loyal to a company that helps them contribute to social and environmental issues."[9] 80% of all consumers believe they are making a personal positive impact on the world when they buy products from purpose-led companies. And 83% of consumers believe companies must prove their positive impact if they are to earn a profit.[10]

These aren't alternate facts. These consumer trends will directly affect what people choose to buy, which should refocus your decisions around how to reimagine your business's role in a world where success is defined by your positive contribution to society. The good news is that there are forward thinking leaders from startups to established companies who, like Ravi Kumar and Infosys, are helping shift momentum toward the societal value motive while providing useful lessons about how your company can adapt.

Norrsken, a Swedish organization founded in 2016, has an ambitious aspiration. With the UN's 17 Sustainable Development Goals as a guide, Norrsken aspires to help entrepreneurs integrate responsible practices in their pursuit of solving the "world's biggest challenges to 'radically improve the world'."[11] They want to create "impact unicorns," which are businesses that positively impact 1 billion people, contrasted with technology unicorns, which are businesses valued at $1 billion.[12] Its investment fund, Norrsken VC, ties partner compensation to the positive impact beyond financials that its portfolio companies have. Since measurable ESG (Environment, Social, and Governance) targets are imprecise, Norrsken invites people to make their impact reports better by, in effect, group sourcing public input. While still early, Norrsken VC's portfolio companies are already having a positive impact:[13]

- Submer Technologies reduced data center energy demand by 10 gigawatt hours using a cooling technology they developed that reduces water usage by 99%, energy consumption by 50%, and occupies 85% less space.

- Four startups – Karma, Whywaste, Matsmart, and Olio – reduced food wasted by 11,000 tons and $CO_2$ emissions by 25,000 tons.

- Alight produced 38 megawatts using solar power (each megawatt can power approximately 190 homes).[14]

Developing your aspiration drives meaning for your business, casting a halo over your societal contribution activities. McKinsey (2020) found that 82% of employees say it is important to have a purpose and 72% want purpose to receive more weight than profit.[15] Around 74% of LinkedIn members seek work that delivers a sense of purpose (2016).[16] Also, 63% of employees say they are motivated when their company clearly defines and communicates how they create value (2019).[17] And a Mercer study (2018) revealed that the "highest-performing employees are 3✕ more likely to work for a company with a strong sense of purpose."[18]

Defining your aspiration is a crucial first step toward building a business that becomes a force for good and delivers positive, measurable value creation. There are three components:

1. Defining your company's *Ultimate Dream*

2. *Creating Value* based on your Ultimate Dream

3. Demonstrating your aspiration through your company's *Character*

## DEFINING YOUR COMPANY'S ULTIMATE DREAM

Each of us harbors dreams about the future and our role in it. Think of "ultimate dream" as your company's positive contribution to society; its *implicit* cause. Maximizing profits and enhancing shareholder value are *not* ultimate dreams; they are obsolete, soulless twentieth century concepts lacking inspiration that aren't meaningful or motivating to employees. People want businesses that contribute to better lives, not just better products. As a leader you have to take on the anxiety-inducing burdens of helping employees see that, despite challenges, your company needs their very best contributions to achieve its aspiration. Your employees are far more likely to start each day excited if you work with them to define and share an ultimate dream that sustains the bright light of hope even in dark times.

Most of the business leaders in my research and work are energized by defining their businesses aspiration (hint: it's more than just making money). What these more enlightened leaders are excited about is making progress toward something *meaningful*. Indra Nooyi, former CEO of PepsiCo, said

> The blind pursuit of profit at all costs is untenable. It is essential that we make money the right way. After all, if communities suffer as a result of a company's actions, those returns are not sustainable.[19]

Yet we have been bombarded during our business careers with messages reinforcing the importance of a "how did you make money for me today?" mentality and are skeptical of *doing good* aspirations. Making money is important but it's how we make money and the decisions we make for reinvesting that money that are of far greater importance. Gartner research shows that 74% of employees expect their companies have a voice in societal issues and that the percentage of highly engaged employees who contribute discretionary effort increased from 40% to 60% when their companies made an active effort to have an outsized impact on the world.[20] Being clear on your company's ultimate dream will catalyze your people to achieve impact based on the good it represents.

The Global Fashion Agenda (GFA) is a not-for-profit organization devoted to supporting a sustainable fashion economy. Formed in 2018 through the collective action of Nike, H&M Group, Asos, Kering, Target, Allbirds, and VP Partners, GFA is pursuing their ultimate dream of changing the way their industry does business. Fashion produces 4% of greenhouse gas emissions and 20% of industry water pollution globally. The GFA encourages new business models aimed at reducing global demand for diminishing resources to keep them "within planetary boundaries," a noble pursuit. McKinsey is the GFA's strategic knowledge partner and the GFA collaborates with Reverse Resources, BGMEA, P4G, and over 30 brands, manufacturers and recyclers dedicated to creating a circular fashion waste model.[21] The GFA's ultimate dream articulates their societal ambitions and represents a growing trend of companies defining their success based on a more responsible business model.

## Ultimate Dream Actions

If you have a nagging anxiety about what your company must do to define its ultimate dream, then do this:

1. Think deeply about the heart and soul of your company. Company cynics often ridicule reflection of this kind, suggesting this is mere naval gazing and is outside the purview of "serious business." But the world is facing serious challenges, business-as-usual won't fix the problems, so deliberate self-reflection will be invaluable for defining your company's ultimate dream. For years there has been a shortage of tech and digital talent worldwide, including in India and the United States, so Infosys reflected on how to build large talent pools in these areas.

2. Discuss the ultimate dream with your stakeholders to gain their input. This is hard work, but so is becoming a force for good, winning an Olympic medal, or developing a successful product. It won't happen overnight, but it also won't happen at all if you don't put in the work. Infosys knew that part of society's prosperity depended on a world where people understood digital technology, hence Ravi's efforts.

3. Actively share and seek insights with your stakeholders. Each conversation strengthens your ultimate dream muscle, much like an athlete training for competition. You may not embrace every idea but the energy you put forth will increase their advocacy for your business. Infosys spent time in the United States learning from stakeholders what skills were needed where. Led by Ravi, the company set up innovation hubs in places with robust academic ecosystems, focusing on non-STEM students, postulating that the future of work depended not just on math and science prowess but also on people who are good problem finders. People with non-STEM experience bring a unique perspective that enriches the problem-finding capability.

4. Co-create action steps with your employees to operationalize your ultimate dream, translating it to each department and business area, celebrating small wins to build organizational confidence. This will help create a movement that inspires more people to join in. Reinforce that everyone is expected to be part of the solution and build momentum as the organization gains experience. Infosys knew from its own employees that the pandemic accelerated digital needs and would likely radically alter workstreams and even entire sectors, catalyzing the company's education efforts further.

5. Distill your stakeholder conversations into key themes. Tell the story of how the ultimate dream came to be, highlighting examples from the conversations. Infosys gained insights about the kinds of skills different academic ecosystems developed, so they initiated partnerships with liberal arts and design schools.

6. Measure impact wherever possible. Like Norrsken, while not everything can be measured easily, do your best to determine what evidence demonstrates progress. And don't shy away from asking for measures you need but can't yet easily formulate. Keeping those known unknowns at the forefront of your meetings may one day lead to a breakthrough. Infosys set an initial target of 10,000 jobs in 2017, which increased to 25,000 jobs by 2022. There is more demand than supply so the pace of digital and tech job creation is likely to continue for years to come.

Take these actions since you don't want to wake up a few short years from now with your company in steep decline as smarter and more responsible competitors zip past you because they made the effort to adapt to the needs of a finite resource world.

## CREATING VALUE BASED ON YOUR ULTIMATE DREAM

The ultimate dream is your company's implicit cause. The *explicit* expression of that cause is the overt value your business creates for society. Creating value has traditionally been described as producing goods and services for customers better than your competitors can while earning superior returns for shareholders. The past century witnessed an explosion of businesses worldwide competing to outperform their competitors, which increased demand for the underlying resources needed to produce ever more products and the corresponding infrastructure development required for moving goods and monies around the world to satisfy the insatiable demand as economies grew. The definition of a successful life in mature economies became inseparable from having an overaccumulation of *things*. As companies grew, so too did shareholder expectations of increasing returns for the stock they owned. To keep growing faster, companies acquired other companies, added international locations, increasing demand for scarce resources from fossil fuels to rare earth minerals to water to land to...well, you get the idea. Smaller businesses followed their far larger brethren, mirroring their models. We now know that the past 100+ years of personal accumulation, business growth, and economic value creation have come at a cost: we are consuming 50% more resources than can be replenished. We will be unable to keep upping the value creation game as the supply of resources declines toward zero while the volume of catastrophic environmental crises rises. That's not a very attractive future.

What can you do about it? Completely overhaul how your business creates value. This is where most business leaders hit a wall because the effort to reimagine-restructure-re*whatever* your business is expensive and incredibly difficult. Plus, we have been told there are few financial rewards from such an undertaking. But is that really true? In a 2015 article reviewing over 2000 empirical studies from the 1970s onward by Gunnar Friede, Timo Busch, and Alexandar Bassen, the authors sought to answer how ESG investments impacted corporate financial performance. Their analysis was clear: 62.6% of the 2000+ studies showed positive findings whereas only 8% had negative findings.[22] In other words, ESG investments create societal gain.

What is the new definition of creating value? It's now about creating *societal good*. I am not hinting to abandon capitalism in favor of socialism. Of all the economic systems in the world, capitalism remains the best for stimulating innovation, allocating capital, and rewarding hard work. But there was a time a few decades ago when companies demonstrated greater concern for employees, including providing pensions. In the United States in 1960, more than half of all private sector employees had pensions, also known as defined *benefits* plans. By the early 1980s, these gave way to defined *contribution* plans, like 401(k), where the employee is responsible for the contributions and the employer can choose whether to offer a limited match. At the same time, capitalism shifted increasingly toward enriching shareholders at the expense of society at large and, at its worst, has led to crony capitalism and extreme wealth disparities where the world's top 1% own twice as much as the bottom 90%.[23] You can't sensibly argue that this is defensible or sustainable for a healthy global society. We need to incentivize businesses to embrace the societal value motive.

Eric Almquist et al. (2016) identified 30 elements of value, synthesized from 30 years of consumer research.[24] The 30 elements of value are allocated across four categories from highest to lowest need:

- Social impact (self-transcendence)

- Life changing (such as belonging, provides hope, etc.)

- Emotional (such as rewards me, fun, wellness, etc.)

- Functional (such as saves time, reduces risk, quality, etc.)

Satisfying social impact is the ultimate area of need and means elements from some or all of the other three areas of value are being met as well. You can see how the value sequence grows from basic personal utility to societal gain. Your definition of value may differ, but Almquist's insights give you a structure for identifying where your company's value contribution resides, from which you can build corresponding "force-for-good" changes into your transformation plans.

## Creating Value Actions

Think of creating value as the by-product of a business ecosystem wherein the participants have agreed upon areas of interest designed to positively impact society. This imposes self-reinforcing systemic expectations about how each partner will uphold their part of the ecosystem. Ask the following of your business and its ecosystem participants:

1. What kind of value are your creating? How does it offer *more*, or *better*, or *different* positive societal impact?

2. What are the kinds of resources (people expertise, technical capabilities, economic) you need to ensure positive societal impact is created?

3. What obstacles are in the way of improving how you create value for society? Are they internal to your business or those of your partners? Are they structural characteristics associated with your competitive arena?

4. What are the underlying causes of those obstacles and what responsibilities must be defined to help partners overcome them?

## DEMONSTRATING YOUR ASPIRATION THROUGH YOUR COMPANY'S CHARACTER

Character is how your business's moral quality is perceived by people in the marketplace. Character is not a glib adjective like "determined" or "innovative." Those kinds of assertive terms may sound impressive but amount to little more than fodder for social media jokes. Instead, your company's character is guided by its ultimate dream and its approach to creating value. Character is built, lived, and exemplified by the people within and then experienced by people outside through their direct interactions with you and the indirect perceptions of others. Why would any business want to be known for having a flawed character or hiring and retaining people with questionable behaviors? While angelic perfection and altruism are unreasonable expectations, especially since businesses have raw edges and people within make mistakes, how you address shortcomings determines whether the market forgives or flays your company. Therefore, character matters. If your company makes a promise, then deliver on it. If it fails, then you better overdeliver on your correction. No organization will survive long if character flaws are not fixed.

### Doconomy and Ålandsbanken

You might not have heard of Doconomy and Ålandsbanken, but why should you, unless you are from Sweden where they are based. There is a 100-year age difference between these two companies (Ålandsbanken [Bank of Åland] was founded in 1919 and Doconomy was founded in 2018), yet they share a common interest in creating societal value and are partnering to reduce our carbon footprint.

Ålandsbanken was founded by farmers and sea captains with a "can do" ethos. Origin stories like this exude authenticity and run counter to the slick corporate descriptions from larger banks that preach security and safety yet come across as soulless. Ålandsbanken's values are incorporated within their Code of Conduct and include a focus on long-term sustainability in financial and ESG areas. A financial focus is understandable; they are a bank, after all. But integrating ESG into their codes of conduct conveys the importance they attach to their societal impact beyond narrow banking practices.[25]

Doconomy's purpose is ambitious: *to future proof life on earth*. Under the guise of "Everyday Climate Action," Doconomy has developed digital tools that show consumers the carbon footprint of each purchase they make, reflecting the company's interest in reducing carbon impact.[26] Their core values focus on

- Care for the environment by helping people take responsibility for their consumption

- Use of money as a force for good

Doconomy and Ålandsbanken came together to create the Åland Index, which measures a consumer's consumption-level carbon impact. By using special credit cards with ecosystem partners consumers get itemized carbon impact metrics of their purchases, with the goal of shifting their spending from high carbon to low carbon purchases.[27]

## Character Actions

1. Survey and validate your known characteristics through stakeholder feedback.

2. Assess how your company's character is perceived by the market and key stakeholders. Does this help you attract talent? If yes, then how do you know? If no, then what actions must you take to fix this?

3. Revisit your approach to hiring and developing people. CVs and interviews are rarely illuminating. There are innumerable more useful ways to hire talent.

- Consider inviting prospective hires to a company and/or stakeholder gathering to see how they relate to others.

- Give prospective hires 24 hours to develop ideas for solving an existing challenge and then have them present their recommendations without using PowerPoint.

4. Once hired, approach their development differently. To illustrate:
   - Integrate ultimate dream, creating value and character attributes into each person's development plan.

   - Don't conduct annual performance reviews. Do regular check-ins instead. Include mentoring and reverse mentoring with different people to gain diverse perspectives.

5. Regularly review wins and losses with employees in different forums. Doing so helps reinforce transparency as essential to your company's character. The more this is done, the more employees will organically share these insights with colleagues, which can help shift a company culture from "that's not what we do around here" to "that's how we learn and improve around here."

## So What?

You now have the blueprint for developing your company's aspiration. The evidence that all of us are living in a world of converging, unprecedented crises is persuasive. Defining your business's aspiration is the first step in reimaging how your company can and must contribute to a healthier society. The three components of aspiration – ultimate dream; creating value; and character – have prescribed actions you can take to get your business prepped for transformation. This matters because the absence of a clear aspiration that focuses people's attention and energies means your company will struggle mightily against smarter and more societally aware competitors. Defining your aspiration helps identify what makes you distinctive, as you'll see in Chapter 2.

## NOTES

1. Du Bois, W. E. B. (1903). The souls of black folk. W.E.B Du Bois Center. Retrieved from http://duboiscenter.library.umass.edu/du-bois-quotes/.
2. Based on 2021 author interviews with Ravi Kumar.

3. No author. (2017). Best global brands. Interbrand, p. 9, citing Havas Media Group 2015 – Havas' meaningful brands study. Retrieved from https://www.interbrand.com/wp-content/uploads/2018/02/Best-Global-Brands-2017.pdf.
4. Daschle, A. (2019). Set your cultural aspiration with these four steps. McKinsey. Retrieved from https://www.mckinsey.com/business-functions/organization/our-insights/the-organization-blog/set-your-cultural-aspiration-with-these-four-steps.
5. Keller, V. (2015). The business case for purpose. EY Beacon Institute. Harvard Business Review, p. 16. Retrieved from https://assets.ey.com/content/dam/ey-sites/ey-com/en_gl/topics/digital/ey-the-business-case-for-purpose.pdf.
6. O'Brien, D., Main, A., Kounkel, S., & Stephan, A. R. (2019). Purpose is everything. Deloitte Insights. Retrieved from https://www2.deloitte.com/us/en/insights/topics/marketing-and-sales-operations/global-marketing-trends/2020/purpose-driven-companies.html.
7. Multiple sources: (1) Bright, A. (2020). 10 of the most socially responsible companies & brands to model. GrownEnsemble. Retrieved from https://growensemble.com/socially-responsible-companies/; (2) No author. (2018). How can sustainability enhance your value proposition? Nielsen. Retrieved from https://www.nielsen.com/wp-content/uploads/sites/3/2019/05/sustainable-innovation-report.pdf.
8. Arnett, H. (2020). The power of a purpose-driven brand (and how to build one). Black&White. Retrieved from https://medium.com/black-white-studios/the-power-of-a-purpose-driven-brand-and-how-to-build-one-26523e66db51.
9. No author. (2016). Cone communications millennial employee engagement study. A Porter Novelli Company. Retrieved from https://www.conecomm.com/research-blog/2016-millennial-employee-engagement-study.
10. Aziz, A. (2020). Global study reveals consumers are four to six times more likely to purchase, protect and champion purpose-led companies. Forbes. Retrieved from https://www.forbes.com/sites/afdhelaziz/2020/06/17/global-study-reveals-consumers-are-four-to-six-times-more-likely-to-purchase-protect-and-champion-purpose-driven-companies/?sh=70ee8299435f.
11. No author. (2021). Norrsken Foundation website. Our Mission. Retrieved from https://www.norrsken.org/ourmission.
12. No author. (2021). Norrsken culture deck (powerpoint). Retrieved from https://docs.google.com/presentation/d/1O3ZEmF_7-tZ77vB0-ZP6LNRk5tza GvYU498C1D50XVY/edit#slide=id.g36732efca1_0_0. Slides 16–19, 128–143.
13. Shieber, J. (2021). To improve accountability, Norrsken VC ties partner compensation to its portfolio's sustainability successes. TechCrunch. Retrieved from https://techcrunch.com/2021/03/28/to-improve-accountability-norrsken-vc-ties-partner-compensation-to-its-portfolios-sustainable-successes/.
14. No author. (2020). Solar Energy Industries Association. 17.7 million homes could be powered by the current installed solar capacity in the US. Retrieved from https://www.seia.org/initiatives/whats-megawatt.
15. Gast, A., Pablo, I., Nina, P., Bill, S., & Bruce, S. (2020, April). Purpose: Shifting from why to how. McKinzey. Retrieved from https://www.mckinsey.com/business-functions/organization/our-insights/purpose-shifting-from-why-to-how.

16. No author. (2016). Purpose at work, 2016 Global report. LinkedIn and ©Imperative, p. 24. Retrieved from https://business.linkedin.com/content/dam/me/business/en-us/talent-solutions/resources/pdfs/purpose-at-work-global-report.pdf.
17. No author. (2019). Business of purpose. Retrieved from https://www.businessofpurpose.com/statistics.
18. See footnote 17.
19. No author. (2014). PepsiCo performance with purpose sustainability report 2014, p. 2. Retrieved from https://www.pepsico.com/docs/album/sustainability-report/2014-csr/pep_csr14_sus_overview.pdf?sfvrsn=efee4f64_4.
20. No author. (2020). Improve the employee experience-create and deliver a high-ROI employee experience. Gartner. Retrieved from https://www.gartner.com/en/human-resources/insights/employee-experience?utm_medium=promotion&utm_campaign=RM_GB_2021_HRL_NPP_MP1_EMPLOYEE-EX-CH.
21. No author. (2020). Global Fashion Agenda. Retrieved from https://www.globalfashionagenda.com.
22. Friede, G., Timo, B., & Alexander, B. (2015). ESG and financial performance: Aggregated evidence from more than 2000 empirical studies. *Journal of Sustainable Finance & Investment, 5*(4), 210–233. Retrieved from https://www.tandfonline.com/doi/full/10.1080/20430795.2015.1118917.
23. O'Brien, P. (2020). World's richest 1 percent own twice as much as the bottom 90 percent. *Philanthropy News Digest.* Retrieved from https://philanthropynewsdigest.org/news/world-s-richest-1-percent-own-twice-as-much-as-bottom-90-percent.
24. Almquist, E., John, S., & Nicolas, B. (2016). The elements of value. *Harvard Business Review.* Retrieved from https://www.hbsp.harvard.edu/product/R1609C-PDF-ENG?Ntt=value+creation&itemFindingMethod=Search.
25. No author. (2021). Ålandsbanken. Retrieved from https://www.alandsbanken.com/.
26. No author. (2021). Doconomy. Retrieved from https://doconomy.com/.
27. No author. (2021). The Åland Index. Retrieved from https://doconomy.com/services/#alandindex.

# 2

# PURSUING DISTINCTION

*We must believe that we are gifted for something, and that this thing, at whatever cost, must be obtained.*[1]

—*Marie Curie*

Growing up in the Philippines, Janice Lao lived in a society where family and community ties are crucial. Early on she witnessed the critical role business plays in a society's social fabric and, simultaneously, dispiriting inequality. As a child she had a paralyzing fear of math, but that did not dissuade her from figuring out how to overcome it. Furthermore, her Jesuit education taught her the value of social justice and a determination to help others by fixing intractable problems. As an adult, she developed a methodology for STEM education, focusing on it as a lifestyle that could spark creativity. She also developed a mathematical and economic model for the aviation industry's carbon-neutral strategy, as well as standard-setting sustainability solutions for carbon trading, biodiversity, textile upcycling, and even refugee hiring practices. Today she is a leading Environmental Scientist and Development Economist serving as ESG Director for a large consumer products company and has been recognized for her achievements, including being awarded the Edie Sustainability Leader of the Year Award in 2019, becoming the first Asian and youngest recipient. Her work has made her a distinctive voice in today's sustainability movement and a role model for leveraging one's work and determination into a force for good that benefits society. When talking to audiences her approach is more of an invitation to join an effort to do right rather than a lecture on what we're doing wrong. As she says, "I don't want you to feel guilty. I DO want you to feel empowered...."[2]

To borrow from Janice, if your company lacks a clear distinction, I don't want you to feel hopeless. Instead, I want you feeling motivated to define the qualities that make your business distinctive. When your company's uniqueness is recognized by the market, then awareness of your business increases and your reputation grows.

Like Janice, many people have had periods in their lives when they were recognized for a distinctive talent or a standout accomplishment that elevated their reputation, and that same transcendent impact arises when businesses use their aspiration to develop distinctive solutions that create positive societal value. The great companies for the remainder of the twenty-first century will require imaginative thinking and courageous actions to challenge business norms. Just as Janice overcame her fear of math, executives and their companies can overcome their fear of changing business models and their own behaviors, forging the path to distinction. Perhaps your business's distinction is obvious to you, but is it understood by your stakeholders?

Claiming uniqueness is different from demonstrating it. Actions speak louder than words. The marketplace is quick to sniff out pretenders and I've seen businesses try to fake their way toward a reputation for being distinctive. A few years ago I was invited by a rapidly growing branded fashion company to visit with their CEO and leadership team to discuss how to improve their reputation. Part of their plan was to apply for an annual award known as the "Most Promising Brand." Submissions required candidate companies to complete a detailed questionnaire, citing evidence of their successful practices. During the meeting I asked their team to provide examples. They didn't have any. They had grown quickly but so too had culture toxicity. They said, "we just want you to help us describe what we do that casts us in a favorable light." I told them deserving award recipients don't whitewash; they practice what they preach. I thanked them for inviting me but declined to help them. When your company genuinely pursues bettering society, you will have a distinctive advantage over competitors stranded by a fixed mindset on an ever-shrinking island of obsolete business practices. According to PwC's Strategy&, companies that identify and leverage their unique factors are "3 times as likely to grow faster than their industry ... are 2.5 times as likely to be more profitable than the market ... (will) make deals that generate 14 percentage points more in annualized total shareholder return."[3]

ACE provides a strategic framework for developing your company's sustained distinction: Achieve, Choreograph, and Enable.

## ACHIEVE

Articulate what you aim to accomplish and be prepared to adjust as the context changes. When I was growing up I kept a copy of an old Track & Field News in my room with a cover photo of Steve Prefontaine ("Pre"). You might not have heard of Pre, but he was the US' best middle-distance runner in the early-mid 1970s before he died in a car accident. He never lost a race during his college years and set American records in every race from 2,000 to 10,000 meters. I wanted to be as good as Pre. I never came close. I wasn't even the best middle-distance runner on my high school track team. Now, you might say that not being as good as Pre means I failed to achieve. But not matching Pre didn't discourage me from running; my context for success changed. What I realized is running was a means to an end, and that end was not to copy Pre but to achieve lifelong health and it sparked an insatiable curiosity for running in new places, having logged more than 60,000 miles in over 40 countries.

Achieving distinction and attaining a particular aim, like Patagonia being known for sustainable clothing or Janice Lao being known for developing the airline industry's carbon-neutral economic model, does not happen because of a perfectly planned linear path of flawless accomplishments. Patagonia floundered in the early 1990s, laying off workers and losing access to credit. That compelled founder Yvon Chouinard to adjust by aligning more closely with environmental causes and pursuing profit with purpose.[4] Patagonia is now known for its distinctive sustainability focus. Janice Lao's youthful struggles with math didn't discourage her; they energized her to show how math sparks ingenious, creative solutions that benefit society. To transform your company don't go nuts developing a several hundred-page plan. Instead, use your aspiration as a catalyst to describe what will be better about your company and its impact on society when you achieve it.

## CHOREOGRAPH

Identify the moves you need to make and who is involved in making them. COVID-19 and the Delta variant have changed the world. During such unprecedented times, the actions you take to achieve your distinction will undoubtedly be different since people are working differently. You must reexamine budget and investment assumptions to protect your force for good transformation objectives. You'll need to actively monitor changing market conditions and customer patterns. You'll need to decide what to do if supply chain disruptions continue. You'll need to determine more effective collaboration methods for remote working. You'll need to coordinate and align with ecosystem partners to ensure your respective activities still support the distinction you seek. You'll need to keep all stakeholders informed about your ongoing pandemic response. Your company's core aspiration won't change; just the way you choreograph the actions on your path to achieving it. Patagonia knew what was needed to achieve distinction; the path they took was contrary to common business practice, including sharing research with competitors and telling customers to consume less. Janice Lao is not telling companies to abandon making and selling products or forgo profits. Instead, her work as an environmental scientist and development economist helps for-profit companies understand the different actions they can take to improve their environmental footprint and market performance.

## ENABLE

Make it easier for people to get things done. Modern society has bred a sense of urgency and impatience in us. Wealth creation and tough-mindedness are celebrated as virtues. Yet those also contain the seeds of disharmony and organizational toxicity. It is tempting to continue the hard-charging business practices of the past few decades simply because they worked in the past. But that's irresponsible and bad for society. First, who wants to work for a jerk? Second, who wants to live in a world rife with environmental destruction, extreme social tensions, and increasingly frequent health crises? Third, past practices often *hamper* getting things done easily because they were developed in an era with different needs. Assess processes and procedures *now* to determine which to STOP and what to START and CONTINUE. Cultural and environmental activism is part of Patagonia's DNA, and the company wants independently minded employees to help improve on its reputation. Managers ensure employees have the right resources and employees are trusted to figure out how to get things done. They are guided by a clear expectation: do what is right. Janice Lao is empowering companies by arming them with information and tools they can then use for improving their sustainability.

Transforming a business is hard. Start by keeping your rationale simple, even though the underlying implications are loaded with complexity. Winning over stakeholders requires that they understand what's at stake for them. You can Google countless articles about how to build a brand that is clearly understood by all stakeholders. While possibly useful, most are derived from overly structured business school frameworks. You want to get things done and not feel like you're prepping for the GMAT. The 3A3D model distills practices I've observed, outlining the essentials you'll need to execute in making your company distinctive:

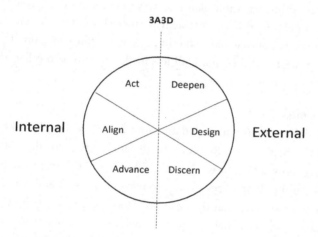

*Source:* John A. Davis, 2001–2021.

## Internal

A crisis shouldn't have to motivate your company to adopt a more responsible business model since there is evidence that ESG-focused companies outperform their non-ESG counterparts. But since most businesses still operate using a twentieth century logic, then a crisis is as good a time as any to reimagine your business.

*Act* with urgency

We tend to see businesses as ponderous, slow-moving elephants incapable of transforming into cheetahs. Yet the rapid development of the

COVID-19 vaccines by pharmaceutical giants Moderna, Pfizer, Johnson & Johnson, and AstraZeneca demonstrated cheetah-like urgency in a time of crisis. But when COVID-19 decreases to a fraction of its current threat, other global crises will persist, so the new normal will be perpetually abnormal. Stop doing the same old thing and start your new business model transition. Evidence shows growing consumer and employee preferences for ESG-focused companies and the financial benefits that accrue.

*To Do:*
Map out a transformation plan that sets time-bound objectives for major product, operational and ecosystem partner shifts. Use design thinking's test and learn approach to experiment where you can gain the highest leverage fastest and then share all lessons learned to help other aspects of your transformation efforts.

*Align* your messaging
Crises heighten attention on you and your company. People want to know how you will respond. Reinforce with employees why the changes are occurring, how jobs and workflows will change, and what the long-term benefits will be. Employees expect your company to stand for something and want reassurance that the business is looking out for them, so let them know that you need their support to achieve the company's aspiration. Gallup research (2017) showed that improvement of 10% in employee understanding of their company's purpose resulted in a 12.7% decrease in safety incidents, 8.1% lower turnover, and 4.4% higher profitability.[5]

*To Do:*
Use *review, rinse, and repeat* to *align* messaging internally:
*Review*: Evaluate current communications and their relevance to your aspiration.
*Rinse*: Clean out old communications and replace with new messages.
*Repeat*: Regularly repeat new messages in different company forums.
Ask employees for their input on how to invest everyone in the transformation.

*Advance* your impact
A business's impact should be felt the same by people inside and outside your company. The market will brand you based on its experience with

you, either positively or negatively. When employees believe their work has meaning, they become genuine advocates for the company and their productivity increases. Janice Lao brings deep ESG experience, having worked previously in similar capacities for Hong Kong and Shanghai Hotels, Cathay Pacific, Swire Pacific, and the World Resources Institute. As the planet heats up, she knows that companies are being scrutinized for their sustainability practices and must demonstrate meaningful advances they have made. The company where she works now issued new ESG guiding principles in February 2021 that apply to all operations and suppliers and are overseen by the Board of Directors. As part of this effort, Janice reports regularly to the Board on their ESG progress. Her company exemplifies the type of serious pivot businesses must make to become a force for good.

*To Do:*

Personalize the outcomes expected from your transformation to each stakeholder by connecting their respective interests to the transformation objectives (i.e., "reduce supply waste by X%"; "commit to X hours of local community support activities"; "reduce your carbon footprint by X amount"; "increase financial outcomes by X%"; etc.).

## External

A crisis is a compelling reason to tell the market why you will pursue business not-as-usual:

*Deepen* your societal engagement

Research indicates that people want companies to be more engaged in society. In 2020, 78% of global customers (consumer and business) said that the pandemic should spur business improvement, 90% said how companies respond will determine their trustworthiness, and 95% said that when trust is nurtured it will increase their chances of being loyal. Furthermore, 66% of customers expect companies to understand their needs, and 52% want personalized offers to reflect the understanding companies have.[6] In the United States, 52% of consumers over 60 years old and 60% under 34 years want companies to be socially responsible.[7] But beware of not fully following through. In 2017, AT&T was given a perfect score by the Human Rights Campaign's Corporate Equality Index (CEI).[8] But then it was revealed the company had donated over $2.7 million to 193 anti-gay politicians.[9] That's careless coordination, smacks of disingenuous intent, and erodes trust with the customers whose needs they are supposed to understand. 2018 research calculated a roughly $75 billion cost to businesses in the United States that had poor customer engagement, and the total worldwide is undoubtedly higher.[10]

*To Do:*

Identify what you must learn from customers to optimize time with them. Get your executives and non-customer facing employees in front of customers as a regular practice to both ask the questions and observe their behaviors. Share the insights learned with the rest of your company. Form diverse customer councils for them to share their views. This will signal that their input matters and will help improve loyalty. Encourage employees to watch for emerging trends and regularly share these insights. Track this information in a database for easy access and ongoing analysis.

*Design* sustainable solutions

Deepening your societal engagement helps determine what changes you need to make to create sustainable solutions. Early in my career I was with Nike's Outdoor group, which made products for hiking, cycling, and trail running. Outdoor customers were very different than Nike's core sports consumers. Products had to address the unique needs of demanding outdoor athletes in challenging conditions. A related group was tasked with reducing waste from discarded footwear that added to overburdened landfills. The group conceived of "Regrind" (now called Grind) that recycled used footwear into new materials. Since then, over a billion square feet of sports surfaces have been made from Nike Grind in over 10,000 such projects globally. Zero waste is the long-term goal. Nike has not achieved that yet but has made an important contribution to reducing their environmental impact.[11]

*To Do:*

Link customer insights to specific solutions designs and processes while also tracking the impact of the insights-led changes and corresponding outcomes. Each internal review meeting should show demonstrable progress in customer relationship improvement and societal value initiatives.

Emphasize this as an "act now" routine because insights will quickly become irrelevant as the world changes. Create a regular societal value lessons-learned newsletter (or similar update) that is shared with all employees.

### Discern your unique capabilities

Making the effort to identify and reinforce *your* unique capabilities is vital because it forces you to fully evaluate what makes you distinctive. It's not enough to say you want the best and brightest, or most experienced, or most creative people. What business doesn't? It's what you do with your people that catalyzes your company's unique capabilities. Consider REI, a Seattle-based company dedicated to outdoor sports, with retail and online stores designed to evoke rugged outdoor environments. REI's purpose-led values and environmental advocacy attract customers and employees. Their employees are diverse, smart outdoor enthusiasts that customers seek. The Human Rights Campaign rated REI 90 rating (out of 100) on their LGBTQ Equality scale.[12] More than 45% of its workforce are women. In 2020, Forbes rated them #1 as the best employer for women.[13]

### To Do:

Determine the unique capabilities your company needs to achieve its aspiration. Instill lifelong learning in your culture and identify portfolios of skills that will help your employees over their career, beyond strengthening their domain expertise. Research shows that millennials, for instance, will have up to 16 employers over their professional lifetime. McKinsey (2018) found that between now and 2030, approximately 100 million people will need to find a different occupation.[14] Developing personal capabilities that can translate across different work contexts will be a critical need for businesses.[15]

Natura is a global cosmetics company based in Brazil with a strategic focus on helping positively impact the global climate crisis through its "Commitment to Life, Sustainability Vision 2030." Natura has consistently invested in being sustainable. The company has been carbon neutral since 2007. Its harmful emissions decreased 33% between 2007 and 2013 and another 11% through 2020, and they are tracking with their 2026 objectives of reducing greenhouse gas emissions by 13% more and achieving 25% post-consumer recycled plastic in all of their packaging as part of their plan to have full packaging circularity.[16] Natura is the world's strongest cosmetics brand according to BrandFinance's annual global rankings of brands by sector.[17] Great Place to Work® produces annual surveys about the world's 25 best workplaces and Natura ranked 24th[18] and as an employee said, "I chose Natura for its values and beliefs, its social responsibility. It is a company that puts its people first and looks out for their well-being. And, above all, acts according to its beliefs and statements. I am really proud to belong to this company."[19] Natura has also fostered a deeply committed community of external stakeholders that includes NGOs, governmental agencies, supply chain partners, and even competitors. Wharton's Aline Gatignon and INSEAD's Laurence Capron wrote an article (2020) about Natura's blend of public and private stakeholders, calling it "Open Institutional Infrastructure (OII)" in which the company invests in resources that are also available to their stakeholders. Natura does not demand that stakeholders subsume their corporate objectives under those of Natura. There is potential risk as some stakeholders might take unfair advantage of the arrangement, and such an investment can be expensive since the benefits don't accrue just to Natura, but to their entire stakeholder ecosystem.[20] Traditional businesses might balk at such an approach, but it has reaped long-term benefits for Natura and its stakeholders.

## A Whole Company Effort

Your business's transformation must be a whole company effort, sequenced in stages, with an eye toward achieving systemic change. Success will depend on whether people perceive your efforts as credible. Don't claim something you're not. You can't advertise or "PR" your business into the good graces of society without actually doing the work. That's known as greenwashing and it gets companies into trouble. Italian energy company Eni was penalized just under US$6 million for misleadingly claiming its diesel fuel made from palm oil was green, implying it was healthy for the environment. Not only was their claim false, but also the cultivation of palm oil crops drives deforestation, not an eco-friendly activity. Furthermore, the EU said that by 2030 all palm oil usage will be reduced to zero due to the devastating environmental impact of palm crop farming practices.[21] Non-profits also make egregious claims. The Rainforest Alliance is a large global NGO with a presence in over 60 countries that specializes in certifying a business's sustainability in agriculture, tourism, and forestry. In 2014, it was sued for certifying Chiquita Bananas as sustainable, yet in reality Chiquita was using fungicides and fertilizers in its plantations, contaminating local drinking water, with nitrate levels 10× higher than what is considered safe.[22]

These examples highlight the perils of conveying a false narrative about your business's angelic qualities. The following steps will help strengthen your transformation toward clearer, credible distinction:

1. Describe the two to three main strategic challenges your company faces over the next 2–3 years as it pivots into a force for good.

2. Identify the outcomes you seek and then reverse engineer to determine your transformation steps. Having a "whole business transformation" set of outcomes as a guide will get your company off to a good start.

3. Map your core capabilities to the transformation steps and then determine which additional capabilities are needed, working with stakeholders and partners to integrate these.

4. Don't get caught up just with best practice comparisons as they are often idiosyncratic to the source organization. Establish your own "next practices" that strengthen your current and desired capabilities.

5. For operationalizing and communicating your transformation, focus on your desired future distinction as that's where you're heading. Be open about past practices that won't be needed going forward.

Finally, you are tackling critical issues with the importance and attention they deserve since many of the global crises are existential threats. Therefore, think of your communications plan as a series of sprints (consider 30–40 days per sprint) signaling that your company and its ecosystem partners are investing in making long-term significant changes designed to create measurable and meaningful societal value. The sprints are first steps in resetting market perceptions. Evolve them as you make progress:

*Sprint 1*: Shift stakeholder expectations (full engagement with stakeholders through every channel: townhalls, digital communities, launch event, etc.)

*Sprint 2*: Align all communications, creative, and media (it shouldn't take months to craft a clear stake-in-the-ground position)

*Sprint 3*: Go to market via your strongest communities of stakeholders (since they've been involved from Sprint 1, they will be your biggest advocates initially, so enlist them to help spread the word to their networks)

*Sprint 4*: Refine, expand, adjust, and persist (you will make mistakes; it happens. Have the confidence that this will create long-term benefits for your company and society.)

## So What?

Multiple crises are converging, disrupting every aspect of our lives. Does focusing on your company's distinction stop these from happening? No. But understanding what does, or will, make you distinctive will help your company realize its aspiration and gain widespread credibility from the communities you serve. Knowing how to accurately communicate your distinction helps people understand the work you are doing to be a force for good.

Asking good questions regularly will help you hone-in on your business's distinction. These are a starting point. Add, edit as you need. But keep asking them.

1. What makes your company distinctive?

2. What decision-making routines should you Stop, Start and Continue using as your business transforms?

3. What are your distinct capabilities that you know make your company special and that are recognized by the market?

4. Is your distinction understood internally throughout the entire organization? If not, then get them up to speed.

5. Does your distinction inspire people internally? Stakeholders externally?

6. How will your plan for being distinctive affect internal operating activities?

7. How will your plan for being distinctive help with selecting external ecosystem partners?

8. What communications actions will help reinforce your distinction?

As a distinctive company you're in a stronger position to create a unique culture that attracts the people you need to help your business prosper, as you'll see in Chapter 3.

## NOTES

1. Labouisse, E. C. (1937). Madame curie: A biography. Part 2. (p. 116). Retrieved from https://quotepark.com/quotes/802709-marie-curie-we-must-have-perserverence-and-above-all-confidenc/.
2. Based on 2021 author Interviews with Janice Lao.
3. Capabilities-driven strategy+growth. Strategy& date unknown. Retrieved from https://www.strategyand.pwc.com/gx/en/unique-solutions/capabilities-driven-strategy.html.
4. Haid, P. (2014). How Patagonia went from turmoil to wildly successful by making counter-intuitive moves. Entrepreneur. Retrieved from https://financialpost.com/entrepreneur/how-patagonia-went-from-turmoil-to-wildly-successful-by-making-counter-intuitive-moves.
5. Dvorak, N. (2017). Three ways mission driven workplaces perform better. Gallop Workplace. Retrieved from https://www.gallup.com/workplace/236279/three-ways-mission-driven-workplaces-perform-better.aspx.
6. No author. (2020). State of the connected customer. Salesforce.com research report. Retrieved from https://www.salesforce.com/resources/research-reports/state-of-the-connected-customer/.
7. Nail, J. (2020). The power of the values-based consumer — and of authentic brand values. Forrester. Retrieved from https://www.forrester.com/blogs/the-power-of-the-values-based-consumer-and-of-authentic-brand-values/.
8. No author. (2017). Corporate equality index. Human Rights Campaign Foundation. (p. 7). Retrieved from https://assets2.hrc.org/files/assets/resources/CEI-2017-FinalReport.pdf.
9. Ennis, D. (2019). Don't let that rainbow logo fool you: These 9 corporations donated millions to anti-gay politicians. Forbes. Retrieved from https://www.forbes.com/sites/dawnstaceyennis/2019/06/24/dont-let-that-rainbow-logo-fool-you-these-corporations-donated-millions-to-anti-gay-politicians/?sh=3d9d5f1b14a6.
10. Hyken, S. (2018). Businesses lose $75 billion due to poor customer service. Forbes. Retrieved from https://www.forbes.com/sites/shephyken/2018/05/17/businesses-lose-75-billion-due-to-poor-customer-service/?sh=147317cb16f9.
11. Nike Grind. (2020). FY20 impact report. Retrieved from https://purpose.nike.com/nike-grind#:~:text=Since%20Nike%20Grind's%20beginning%20as,10%2C000%2B%20projects%20around%20the%20world.

12. Chen, C. (2019). How REI has managed to lead with its values and still turn a profit. *BusinessInsider*. Retrieved from https://www.insider.com/rei-company-values.
13. Multiple sources: (1) Stych, A. (2020). REI tops Forbes list of America's best employers for women. *BizWomen*. Retrieved from https://www.bizjour nals.com/bizwomen/news/latest-news/2020/07/rei-forbes-list-best-employers-women.html?page=all; (2) No author. (2020). REI proves digital strategy and values-based business is a winning combination. NCR. Retrieved from https://www.ncr.com/blogs/rei-proves-digital-strategy-and-values-based-busi ness-is-a-winning-combination.
14. Lund, S., Anu, M., James, M., Sven, S., Kweilin, E., Mary, M., & Olivia R. (2021). The future of work after Covid-19. Retrieved from https://www. mckinsey.com/featured-insights/future-of-work/the-future-of-work-after-covid-19.
15. Sloley, C. (2021). The three things millennials want if they are going to work for you. Citywireselector. Retrieved from https://citywireselector.com/news/ the-three-things-millennials-want-if-they-are-going-to-work-for-you/a1455897.
16. No author. (2021). Natura & Co raises US$1 billion in sustainability-linked bond offer. Cision PR Newswire. Retrieved from https://www.prnewswire. com/news-releases/natura-co-raises-us1-billion-in-sustainability-linked-bond-offer-301282631.html.
17. No author. (2021). Cosmetics 50. BrandFinance. Retrieved from https:// brandirectory.com/rankings/cosmetics/.
18. No author. (2021). World's 25 best workplaces. Retrieved from https:// fortune.com/worlds-best-workplaces/.
19. See footnote 18. Retrieved from https://www.greatplacetowork.com/best-workplaces/worldsbest/2017/natura.
20. Gatignon, A., & Laurence, C. (2020). Blending public and private value cre-ation at Natura. Knowledge@Wharton. Retrieved from https://knowledge. wharton.upenn.edu/article/blending-public-private-value-creation-natura/.
21. Multiple sources: (1) Hicks, R. (2020). Eight brands called out for green-washing in 2020. Eco-Business. Retrieved from https://www.eco-business.com/ news/8-brands-called-out-for-greenwashing-in-2020/; (2) Reuters Staff. (2018). EU to phase out palm oil from transport by 2030. Reuters. Retrieved from https://www.reuters.com/article/us-eu-climatechange-palmoil/eu-to-phase-out-palm-oil-from-transport-fuel-by-2030-idUSKBN1JA21F.
22. Shemkus, S. (2014). Better bananas: Chiquita settles lawsuit over green marketing, but the legal battle isn't over. *The Guardian*. Retrieved from https://www.theguardian.com/sustainable-business/2014/dec/19/chiquita-lawsuit-green-marketing-bananas-water-pollution.

# 3

# REINVIGORATING CULTURE

*Be great in act, as you have been in thought.*[1]
— *William Shakespeare, King John*

We try to make business scientific by measuring everything. But to paraphrase Neil deGrasse Tyson, humans make things go nonlinear. We don't always make sense. Enter Chip Conley, one of the best sense-makers in today's business world. Chip and Neil have a lot in common. And Chip has recognized nonlinearity as vital to building successful company cultures and communities. While human nonlinearity undoubtedly caused many of today's global challenges, people also have the capacity to work things out, to find a way, to collaborate toward a common goal.

Chip founded Joie de Vivre Hotels (JDV), was a strategic advisor and mentor at AirBNB, and his newest venture is Modern Elder Academy (MEA), founded in 2018. He believes in karmic capitalism, that "what goes around comes around," and that businesses have a special responsibility to do more to be active in fostering a healthy society, starting with fostering a healthy company culture. At JDV, Chip created an employee pyramid of needs with three themes, borrowing from Maslow. Survival is the pyramid's base and is about money. Success is in the middle, focused on recognition. Transformation is at the peak and is about giving employees meaning. Over the years, JDV went through its up and down cycles, and his pyramid helped focus attention on these core employee needs, strengthening a company culture, especially in tough times, that was widely recognized for its low turnover in an industry infamous for the opposite. JDV's culture was reflected in each of its 50+ utterly unique hotels. If you were to line up each of JDV's properties, you would be convinced each was from a different hotel company.

That was deliberate and contrary to industry practice. Each had a distinct personality catering to unique guest needs (i.e., Hotel Phoenix was the rock and roll hotel, Hotel Rex was for people who loved books, etc.). Chip wanted his hotels to be more than just a unique place to stay. They had to be part of the fabric of their communities, so JDV created cultural ambassadors whose responsibility was to find a local organization to support through the hands-on contributions of its employees. Chip's pyramid of caring for and supporting employee needs was paid forward by employees in how they cared for and supported the communities where they were located. To illustrate, Hotel Phoenix supported musicians suffering from hearing loss and Hotel Rex helped with literacy in San Francisco's Mission District. Years later, during his tenure at AirBNB, Chip leveraged his nearly 30 years of hotel experience to be a mentor to founder Brian Chesky, while also serving as a mentee who learned from people half his age about the world of technology. He imparted wisdom about the world of hospitality, and they imparted wisdom about technology, with the combination further strengthening AirBNB's culture. As AirBNB grew, it became apparent that the company had a unique platform that could be a force for good, helping house refugees (most recently in 2021 with refugees from Afghanistan in 2021), supporting artists in cities, or people who simply needed monthly housing to help them get back on their feet. Throughout the past decade, AirBNB's culture evolved from one defined by technology-driven convenience, to hospitality, to caring for society.

After several years with AirBNB, Chip moved on. But he wasn't done. Ever curious, he was intrigued by the challenge of how wisdom gets shared from one generation to the next and why the conventional life stages of our modern world favored youth, relegating more seasoned generations to insignificance, with society poorer as a result. Modern Elder Academy (MEA), based in Baja, Mexico, was born. MEA is "an academy dedicated to navigating midlife transitions" and was inspired by his realization that while rites of passage accompany many transitions in life, such as school graduations, there are no clear events to mark midlife. MEA is, in essence, a school to "grow whole, not old," offering workshops in which participants (from their 20s to 90s) focus on rejuvenating their work, their ambitions, their lives, and their ways to contribute to the world. Chip and his team provide a very personal approach to MEA program attendees, teaching, giving guidance, and practicing what they preach, all in a relaxed ocean-front setting that allows people to viscerally feel a reconnection to the world and their individual purpose. Chip knows that how he treats his employees impacts how they treat guests, and the experience guests receive will ultimately impact how they make a difference in the world. It turns out MEA tapped into a vast unmet need and has grown quickly. A second campus is being developed near Santa Fe, New Mexico. Each of Chip's business adventures illustrates his nonlinear, experiential approach to business, bringing together employees with customers and society in general, reinforcing that company success results from a healthy company culture.[2]

We can't perfectly predict how people will respond to a specific situation. Your experience within your company affords you a degree of insight to guesstimate how people might behave in select circumstances. But until an event or condition happens, all bets are off. I've taught leaders in dozens of countries, and many believe they can control their company culture as if they are manipulating numbers on a spreadsheet. It doesn't work, because this kind of micro-management thinking is a vestige of the twentieth century hierarchical control business model when only a few people at the top had access to strategic knowledge, developed the business plans, and then told others what to do. The world has since evolved and we've gotten collectively smarter, yet too many companies treat culture in a regressive way, ridding it of any semblance of spark and meaning for employees. At its core the very idea of culture evokes rich imagery, associations, and customs that ignite our senses and distinguish one community from another. Think of another country and you'll likely picture the people, food, the language, and historical landmarks. The same logic applies to how your business is perceived by others. To succeed you'll need to transform your understanding of culture into one that reflects the idiosyncratic values and practices of your company that attracts people to you and provides a means of social-professional connection for your employees. You must be far more involved in energizing a workplace environment that encourages people to live by your business's core values and take agency in contributing to fulfilling its aspiration.

Each year major media outlets like Forbes, Fortune, Glassdoor, and Comparably produce their respective annual rankings of the best companies to work for, highlighting companies that have built vibrant internal cultures. The rankings celebrate attributes that make the workplace enriching and appealing. Conversely, your culture can also lead to a quick death if you don't make the continuous effort to cultivate a shared ethos about why your company's change journey is important. Peter Drucker is credited with saying "Culture eats strategy for breakfast." Your company's pivot to societal contribution will succeed or fail because of the culture you foster. Yet we know that changing company culture is really hard. Consider this question from a personal perspective. How might you react if I said you had to change. You are likely to be defensive, at least initially, because your self-understanding is being challenged. Now imagine how trying to transform a culture could challenge both a person's sense of self *and* social standing within the company. Recent research in *The British Journal of Psychology* suggests that overcoming these threats can be achieved by focusing on the person's values and sense of social and moral engagement, "Humans have a primary psychological need to be valued and included by others, to feel that they are good and appropriate group members or relationship partners... When people do something wrong this primary psychological need is threatened, driving a defensive response.[3] But addressing that psychological need to belong can reduce their defensiveness."[4] When you encourage people to imagine what a better world could be if they banded together to make the changes sought, you shift the conversation away from defending the status quo and their role in it toward that more aspirational state and their contribution to enhancing the culture.

A 2019 Duke CE study of business leaders around the world I co-authored showed that 75% are worried about their company's ability to respond quickly to market changes and seeping cultural toxicity arising from growth pressures burdening employees with intensive demands to be even more productive. During interviews, several CEOs said that while financial performances have improved, internal engagement scores (a measure of employee satisfaction) were declining at an accelerating pace, indicating that aggressive growth had come at the expense of employee health, morale, and well-being. Divergent growth-engagement trajectories aren't sustainable. Employees will leave the soul crushing atmosphere (usually the good ones first). Many CEOs blamed themselves for being insensitive to their company culture, urging their successors to correct these mistakes.[5] In one especially glaring example, an executive proudly showed her company's 5 years of double-digit growth as evidence of their successful strategy. However, the company's engagement scores were decreasing at an increasing rate year over year. Furthermore, her own behavior was cited as a key reason for the alarming scores. Why? She had a reputation for driving employees hard and, when they underperformed, bullying them, behavior that was hardly reflective of what we would want in a Head of People.

In my work with companies in 40+ countries, three ingredients consistently appear in healthy company cultures:

1. A Dynamic *Organizational Fabric*

2. A Love of *Learning* Mindset

3. Admirable *Behaviors*

## A DYNAMIC ORGANIZATIONAL FABRIC

Consider what fabric is. A cloth or tapestry of fibers woven together in such a way that its appearance creates a certain look, feel, and even attitude. Take that same idea and apply it to your company as you transform. Language is an essential thread in your organizational fabric so how it is used matters, and how we describe our companies should, too. You're trying to transform your company to address tomorrow's needs given the global challenges we face, so stop using yesterday's terminology. The term "organizational fabric" evokes a different reaction than organizational chart, or job titles, or lines of reporting. It conjures images of a colorful, rich, and diverse workplace where people are inspired and challenged by each other, and their ideas can flow; where they feel safe in the notion that the company is looking out for them and that it is seeking their best insights from the crazy quilt of people within; and that they won't be humiliated if they make a mistake. Since language does indeed matter, kick start the weaving of your organizational fabric by no longer referring to employees as human capital. That sounds as uplifting as mortuary Olympics. We're not human capital, we're people who are creating the social atmosphere that defines acceptable behavior in our company. While we're at it, let's eliminate other obsolete terms like human resources, personnel, and talent. Each of those dehumanizes people, making them into generic business terms devoid of life.

Internal practices are another vital thread. Developing your company's organizational fabric requires the courage to abandon many previous conventions, adopt new practices to stimulate people, and gain comfort with discomfort as people collectively work to achieve your company's aspiration. Abandon the archaic expectation that people professionals are primarily policy police, as that signals to employees they are not to be trusted. And let's get rid of putting people on probation when first hired or promoted. It sends mixed signals: on the one hand you want them, yet on the other hand you don't trust them. Either bring them in, or don't, but a probationary period is silly and demotivating in most workplaces today. Another practice that is changing is where people should be located. As COVID-19 grew, companies around the world were forced to alter work policies, including location. This changed the global commercial real estate market dramatically, and once the pandemic recedes, it is unlikely most workplaces will return to a pre-pandemic, business-as-usual approach. Not surprisingly, the energy usage and green impact of 2020's global shutdown showed a significant reduction in harmful emissions and commercial energy usage. Of course, there was a huge economic cost, but that paled in comparison to the irreversible loss of human life. Yet the pandemic showed that businesses could still survive without requiring people to commute to corporate offices, emitting harmful carbon along the way and straining global energy grids during peak work hours. You undoubtedly have other practices that aren't fit for purpose. Eliminate them.

## Social Dynamics

You've heard the aphorism that people don't leave bad jobs, they leave bad bosses. A survey by Achievers (2020) showed that 21% of employees view leadership quality as vital to job satisfaction and 45% believe leaders don't walk the culture talk.[6] Leaders must lead, and that includes keeping people motivated, especially when communicating organizational changes as these affect your company's social dynamics. For example, 40% of employees have felt underappreciated by their bosses during the pandemic.[7] This sense of underappreciation is true whether the change is organic (adjusting internally to rapid market changes from the pandemic) or inorganic (adjusting to an M&A integration). 82% of employees seek greater recognition for their efforts, so you can imagine how a crisis or an acquisition can exacerbate this feeling.[8] It's relatively easy to acquire another company, but it's incredibly hard to weave two or more company cultures together. Organizational changes like these can understandably lead employees to feel anxious about their future.

Here are a few takeaways to help as you anticipate the changes ahead for your company:

1. *Communicate. Again and Again*
   Listening to concerns and communicating clearly strengthens your organizational fabric, improving social dynamics. Otherwise, people fill communication gaps with their own stories, which means your overall change narrative gets lost in the cacophony of competing storylines.

2. *Reboard and Onboard Differently*
   Change creates uncertainty for people. You must personalize why the change is occurring and how people fit into the new structure. Reinforce relationship building across the organization through group and 1:1 get-togethers as gaining familiarity with others reduces the tendency to label and stereotype them.

3. *Identify Your Stop, Start, Continue Priorities*
   Regularly revisit organizational practices to update whether they are still relevant. Start, Stop, Continue stimulates employees to discuss openly how to improve the organization.

4. *The Power of the Fishbowl*
   In this case the fishbowl is your company, so imagine how it looks to observers from the outside. How would you describe your company's social dynamics? Is it a healthy environment? Does it create a good impression? What personality traits represent your company's culture? Do you follow through on your promises? What will we do differently to foster a workplace that is less environmentally damaging and better for our employees' health? Your customers and other key stakeholders are always evaluating whether you meet their expectations and in today's hyperreactive social media environment if they perceive a murky workplace, you'll hear about it because those impressions will follow you everywhere until you fix them. Or go out of business.

## A LOVE OF LEARNING MINDSET

For businesses worldwide to become a consistent force for good requires good leaders. And good leaders must be good learners. Gandhi once said "live as if you may die tomorrow, but learn as if you will live forever." While careers are shorter than ever, our lifespans are growing longer. People having upwards of 16 different employers over their working career is a far different pattern than decades ago when the ideal was spending an entire career with a single organization.[9] Numerous crises are changing the context around how we live and work. We can't separate our companies from these events because our businesses are a part of society and are here because society has given us permission to participate and not operate separately from it. In this new world, the role of learning in your company must change as this will help reinvigorate your culture.

A Deloitte study (2020) showed that 86% of companies are investing in improving learning and development (L&D) to upskill employees and keep them interested in their work.[10] A Gartner survey (2018) showed that 57% of employees want just-in-time learning to help them stay current in their skills.[11] This trend of renewed interest in updating L&D is not just about improving content. Tony O'Driscoll, Professor of Practice at the Fuqua School of Business at Duke University, and a leading authority in organizational learning, once said "content is king, but context is the kingdom."[12] Content is ubiquitous; we can access it anywhere on any digital device and platform. The bigger bang for your upskilling buck occurs when you connect the content to the business and global context of the moment and show how that is relevant to your people. With today's changing context, you'll need to change your mindset about how to evaluate people development. Too many organizations are trying to perfectly measure every aspect of their learning because they need to show their boss the ROI, Return on Investment, from training. But that's the wrong approach. Use ROE, Return on Expectation, because it assesses a person's capabilities and contribution to value creation at both the individual and enterprise levels, and ROC, Return on Curiosity, which evaluates the fresh insights a person brings that create meaningful value for the company. Pay it forward to them through tailored, innovative development plans that, in turn, enhance your company's value to them.

Stanford University's d.School started the @Stanford Project (2014), a thought experiment to understand how higher education changed given technology advances and rapidly shifting societal expectations. They created a concept called "Axis Flip" that describes a "from to" change in what a university education could become: shifting from disciplinary topics to skill acquisition; from university domain/academic field expertise to competency hubs; and from transcripts showing academic performance to skill prints that describe a person's capabilities.[13] Axis Flip is a novel idea. Competency hub examples included Scientific Analysis, Quantitative Reasoning, Social Inquiry, Moral and Ethical Reasoning, Aesthetic Interpretation, Creative Confidence, and Communication Effectiveness. The skill prints are described as "building blocks of capabilities that can be continuously developed, rearranged, and translated across a myriad of work contexts throughout a person's life."[14]

Imagine adapting the axis flip concept to your workplace. It could be a significant game changer that helps your company break away from the old school training mindset and toward helping people develop career capabilities that can be applied to a broader array of work challenges by evolving their skill print portfolios as their responsibilities change. Like Stanford's idea of a new type of undergraduate education, professional skill prints would be akin to a person's career fingerprints; a portfolio of capabilities unique to them. Your company would hire predicated partly on a person's skill prints (either from university or a prior employer) and then develop specific building blocks based on work contexts. This approach could help that person be a more engaged, energized contributor to society as their skill print portfolio gains breadth and depth as they progress through their careers.

Ask the following questions about your company's people development expectations:

1. *Is it clear what skills all employees, including senior leadership, must do more of, better, and/or differently for your business transformation to succeed?* This provides a compass heading for the skill print portfolios you'll need.

2. *Do you and your senior leadership team advocate a culture of learning?* Lead by example by sharing insights and participating in developing people.

3. *Does your culture encourage experimentation, share lessons, and able to unlearn?* Unlearning is hard because we carve deep channels of habits that are convenient and automatic.

## ADMIRABLE BEHAVIORS

Back in 1985 I was lucky enough to be given tickets to the Super Bowl game between the San Francisco 49ers and the Miami Dolphins (won by the 49ers 38-16). Apple ran a TV ad introducing the MacIntosh Office that showed a line of business people dressed in gray business suits with blindfolds on, marching off a cliff, like lemmings to the sea. The message was intended to be a humorous poke at the computer companies of that era, known for being slick corporate machines but lacking a sense of individuality. The imagery of behaviorally consistent, identically dressed business people evoked a sense of personal invisibility within a company of bland sameness. The ad was a disaster for Apple, partly because the MacIntosh Office was two years from being ready, but primarily because the message was bleak and depressing. Behaviors that lead to hopeless, robotic uniformity are not the answer to the question of how to transform your company into a force for good.

Demonstrating business behaviors that convey how the work you and your company does is society-enriching and not just company-enriching requires the courage to change the current business success paradigm. This necessitates a mindset shift about business behaviors because we are taught that market growth and profitability are the gold standard determinants of company success, not whether the company displays concern for global crises. McKinsey (2020) said a limiting mindset is an obstacle to change.[15] Keller and Schaninger (2016) said having a clear aspiration improves the chances of transformation success by 300 percent and a key factor is how you and your colleagues behave.[16] MIT (2020) studied 500 companies and found no correlation between a company's stated values and whether employees believed companies actually lived by them.[17] That is startling and indicates leaders aren't practicing what they preach. If you want transformation to succeed, then how you show up and behave matters. One of the great joys of my work has been teaching thousands of managers and spending time with fascinating leaders from around the world. No two people are identical, but hundreds of conversations and surveys identified dozens of characteristics of top performers that fell into five meta-themes I call The Five Ambassadors. Even accounting for individual differences, there is a shared quality that encapsulates the top performers:

A person who consistently exceeds expectations, leads by example, and whose behaviors are admirable and worthy of emulation, thereby representing the very best of society.[18]

Having a strong ethical and moral compass was the minimum entry requirement for a top performer which is why you don't see those qualities explicitly called out. Furthermore, a truly top performer had to demonstrate all Five Ambassador behaviors consistently in their work. Note that being good at fewer than all Five Ambassadors does not mean a person is a poor performer or failure. Far from it. People have very successful careers being a "less-than-five" performer. But those who do well in all five offer particularly interesting lessons as you think about developing your culture for the future.

## The Five Ambassadors

Attributes corresponding with each Ambassador give further definition about the behavior.

| Relationship Ambassador | |
| --- | --- |
| Genuine appreciation that people matter | |
| **Unique Unifier** | **Trust Enabler** |
| Creates belief in pursuing special cause | Encourages respect and openness |
| **Self Reflector** | **Compassion Catalyst** |
| Self-reviews to gain self-understanding | Acts to help others |

| Experience Ambassador | |
| --- | --- |
| Shares wisdom from lifetime of trial and error | |
| **Credibility Creator** | **Others Enricher** |
| Aims to delight, surprise by overdelivering | Helps stakeholders see how they fit in |
| **Imperfection Exemplar** | **Movement Motivator** |
| Serves as model of fallibility, shares lessons | Enthusiastically invites participation |

| Curiosity Ambassador | |
| --- | --- |
| Energetic curiosity about the world | |
| **Insights Seeker** | **Considerate Contrarian** |
| Animated by unanswered questions | Tests understanding before deciding |
| **Shape Shifter** | **Open-Minded Optimist** |
| Willing to adjust as evidence grows | Believes things can improve |

| Imagination Ambassador | |
| --- | --- |
| Encourages exploration and experimentation | |
| **Novel Interpreter** | **Convention Breaker** |
| Uses existing resources in unique ways | Willing to challenge decision making |
| **Choice Voicer** | **Play Dreamer** |
| Seeks multiple pathways and options | Finds creative ways to simulate new ideas |

| Brand Ambassador | |
| --- | --- |
| Embodies organization values and societal contribution | |
| **Story Teller** | **Reputation Endorser** |
| Narrates using verbal and visual imagery | Exemplifies company's values |
| **Complexity Simplifier** | **Meaning Maker** |
| Widens access by being clear, uncomplicated | Connects people to company aspiration |

*Source:* John A. Davis. Research 2000–2021.

### Curiosity Ambassador

They relish gaining deep knowledge of markets and trends, integrating these evidence-based insights into their work. Ask these questions:

1. What is that person's appetite for gathering insights?

2. Are they open to people who challenge them and their worldview?

### Relationship Ambassador

They channel their social energy toward understanding other people and what makes them "tick."

1. Are they able to rally people for a need, cause, initiative?

2. Do they work well with others?

### Imagination Ambassador

They have an out-of-the-box mindset and an appreciation for creativity, even if they personally lack trained creative skills.

1. Do they encourage and inspire others to think creatively?

2. Are they comfortable pushing for opposing perspectives?

### Experience Ambassador

They are an articulate authority of their own experiences and crave that same expertise from others.

1. Is the person secure enough to admit when they are wrong or have failed?

2. Do they invite input and feedback?

### Brand Ambassador

They exude a compelling ability to advocate for their organization, its people, and its image.

1. Is the person able to describe things clearly?

2. Do they help people feel connected to the organization's aspiration?

In a world where selfies, demagogues, and outsized personalities grab our attention, it is refreshing to know there are terrific people around the world we don't know personally but who represent the very best of us and are helping companies become better.

## SO WHAT?

Company culture is a big, complex area for any business and most of us learn the hard way how to determine where we best fit in and if we believe in our company's direction. You can't just mandate change from above and expect people to fall in line. You've got to be willing to led by example and show care for the people in your company if you want to foster the kind of dynamic organizational fabric that inspires a love of learning and encourages admirable behaviors on your path to becoming a force for good. In Chapter 4 we'll show how leveraging aspiration, distinction, and culture creates memorable experiences.

## NOTES

1. Shakespeare, W. (date uncertain. Attributed to mid-1590s to 1623). King John. Act 5. Scene 1. Retrieved from https://www.rsc.org.uk/king-john/about-the-play/famous-quotes.
2. Based on 2021 author Interviews with Chip Conley.
3. Wenzel, M., Woodyatt, L., & McLean, B. (2020). The effects of moral/social identity threats and affirmations on psychological defensiveness following wrongdoing. British Journal of Social Psychology, 59(4), 1062–1081. doi: 10.1111/bjso.12378.
4. Styx, L. (2020). New research explains how to deal with defensive behavior in emotional times. Very Well Mind. Retrieved from https://www.verywellmind.com/how-to-deal-with-defensive-behavior-in-emotional-times-5090103#citation-1.
5. Corboz, A.-V., John D., & Vishal P. (2019). Is your organization ready to shift? Retrieved from https://www.dukece.com/insights/is-your-organization-ready-to-shift/.
6. Laker, B. (2020). 3 reasons why restructures fail and what to do about it. Forbes. Retrieved from https://www.forbes.com/sites/benjaminlaker/2020/03/03/3-reasons-why-restructures-fail-and-what-to-do-about-it/.
7. Baumgartner, N. (2020). 2020 culture report. Achievers, p. 13. Retrieved from https://www.achievers.com/wp-content/uploads/2020/10/Achievers_2020-Culture-Report_Culture-Continuity.pdf.

8. Nobes, C. (2021). Why employee recognition is important and key benefits. *Achievers*. Retrieved from https://www.achievers.com/blog/why-employee-recognition-important-benefits/.
9. Kingl, A. (2020). The price of doing business with Gen Y. LinkedIn. Retrieved from https://www.linkedin.com/pulse/price-doing-business-generation-y-adam-kingl/?trk=public_profile_article_view.
10. Carr, J. (2020). The future of learning: Top five trends for 2020. *Forbes*. Retrieved from https://www.forbes.com/sites/forbeshumanresourcescouncil/2020/03/25/the-future-of-learning-top-five-trends-for-2020/?sh=1970e3e66cd3.
11. George, S. (2018). Fine-tune development spend to make managers more effective. Gartner. Retrieved from https://www.gartner.com/smarterwith gartner/fine-tune-development-spend-to-make-managers-more-effective.
12. O'Driscoll, T. (2007). Learning matters! Web 2.0 and Personal Learning Environments (PLEs). Wadatrip.wordpress. Retrieved from https://wadatripp. wordpress.com/2007/04/13/web-20-and-personal-learning-environments-ples/.
13. No author. (2014). Stanford 2025 Axis Flip. Stanford University d.school. Retrieved from http://www.stanford2025.com/axis-flip.
14. See footnote 13.
15. Craven, M., Fong, A., Lauricella, T., & Tan, T. (2020). The long haul: How leaders can shift mindsets and behaviors to reopen safely. McKinset. Retrieved from https://www.mckinsey.com/business-functions/organization/our-insights/the-long-haul-how-leaders-can-shift-mindsets-and-behaviors-to-reopen-safely.
16. Daschle, A., Jurisic, N., Parsons, J., & Varma, R. (2019). Set your cultural aspiration with these four steps. McKinsey. Retrieved from https://www.mckinsey.com/business-functions/organization/our-insights/the-organization-blog/set-your-cultural-aspiration-with-these-four-steps.
17. Sull, D., Steano, T., & Soll, C. (2020). When it comes to culture, does your company walk the talk? *MITSloan Management Review*. Retrieved from https://sloanreview.mit.edu/article/when-it-comes-to-culture-does-your-company-walk-the-talk/.
18. Davis, J. (2019). The five ambassadors of leadership. *Dialogue Review*. Retrieved from https://dialoguereview.com/five-ambassadors-leadership/.

# 4

# CREATING EXPERIENCES

*Nothing ever becomes real until it is experienced.*[1]

*–John Keats*

*…it was as if time stood still, and I was flooded with both emotion and awareness. But as I looked down at the Earth – this stunning, fragile oasis, this island that has been given to us, and that has protected all life from the harshness of space – a sadness came over me, and I was hit in the gut with an undeniable, sobering contradiction.*

*In spite of the overwhelming beauty of this scene, serious inequity exists on the apparent paradise we have been given. I couldn't help thinking of the nearly one billion people who don't have clean water to drink, the countless number who go to bed hungry every night, the social injustice, conflicts, and poverty that remain pervasive across the planet.*

*Seeing Earth from this vantage point gave me a unique perspective – something I've come to call the orbital perspective. Part of this is the realization that we are all traveling together on the planet and that if we all looked at the world from that perspective we would see that nothing is impossible.*[2]

*–NASA Astronaut Ron Garan*

Welcome to experiences. Or more accurately, the sensation a person feels when they have a profound experience with a person, event, brand, product, or organization. Most of us will never get to do what Ron Garan did, but we can certainly understand and appreciate the sense of awe a powerful experience can have. Having orbital perspective is a great way to view how to develop memorable experiences for your stakeholders. Most of us don't always think about how the world outside our companies is experiencing us, yet the positive impact we could have has enormous potential if we view our work through the orbital perspective of societal value. Fast forward to the future and imagine a world in which your business is revered for the imaginative way it has improved how you and I live. Granted, envisioning your company with the same reverence Ron Garan has for the earth may seem daunting, but that's because we've been socialized to see businesses as producers of goods and profit maximizers for a narrow group of beneficiaries rather than as enablers of a healthier society.

You must understand the magnitude of the crises affecting all of us and act by translating your intellectual awareness into company-wide actions that demonstrate real, practical societal value. If you stand by in the hope your company will emerge one day unscathed, then you're naïve as the evidence is against you, and you're dangerous for society. Acting positively and force-fully will be hard. It will be expensive. It will change how you do business. And it is absolutely necessary. Don't paint pictures promising all the good you believe in while behind the scenes your supply chain partners continue to abuse workers' rights, pollute local waterways, and enable toxic workplace cultures as you'll be found out. That sounds scary, but soft pedaling these existential threats only gives false comfort. Consumers around the world experience your company through its products, among many touchpoints, and they'll know whether the production of those products harmed people or the environment; they'll know if you are greenwashing; they'll know if your workplace is toxic. Those factor into how they experience you. The good news is that, assuming you're like most companies and leaders, you depend on data to make informed decisions and research shows that people want businesses to be more responsible and not just extractors of economic profits that primarily benefit shareholders. You also want to build a movement of supporters, and research shows they are primed for your company to give them a great experience. According to a global PwC survey (2020)[3]:

- A great experience can lead to a ~16% price premium on products and services.

- In the United States, 63% of consumers are willing to share more infor-mation to companies that provide superb experiences and that they trust for being responsible.

- 65% say that a positive experience is more powerful than advertising.

- 49% of Latin American consumers will abandon a company after a bad experience.

- Globally, 32% would leave a company after just one bad experience.

Don't just think about your company's customer experience (CX). Employee experience matters, too. 92% of company HR leaders are prioritizing employee experience for developing their workforces.[4] PwC's Workforce Pulse Survey in 2021 described four critical components for employees[5]:

1. Physical safety: COVID-19 heightened employees' awareness of and concerns for their personal safety at work. They want a workplace and workforce philosophy that protects them.

2. Mental health: Remote work risks the feeling of isolation and will remain an issue that companies must address through ongoing outreach and support programs.

3. Flexible time: Employees prefer having more time over more compensation. GenZ and Millennials will accept lower pay in exchange for greater work flexibility.

4. Understand needs: Monolithic corporate responses are tone deaf. Employees want their employers to listen carefully to their challenges, including increased workloads, and to feel included.

With five generations in today's workplace creating powerful employee experiences requires that you know more about them than their name and title; you must show that you understand generational and diversity differences. Consider technology savviness for example. Gen Z (born after 1996) are digital natives; Millennials (born between 1981 and 1996) came of age as the Internet went from being unknown to indispensable within a few short years; Gen X (born between 1965 and 1980) grew up just as PCs changed how people work; Baby Boomers (born between 1945 and 1964) had to learn how to change from an analog world to a computer and digital one; and the Silent Generation (born between 1928 and 1945) mostly did not work with any of today's technology. The same is true with customers. IBM, a 110-year-old company, understands this. Diane Gherson (2018), the company's former Chief Human Resources, said employee engagement accounts for two-thirds of a customer's experience score, so making the employee's experience vital to your company's success seems like a sensible idea.[6] Furthermore, both customer and employee experiences show evidence of correlation. Creating great CX is correlated with higher employee engagement (they are 1.5 times more engaged).[7] When your employees believe their work is meaningful, then they contribute more discretionary effort that is reflected in the experiences they create for customers. When those experiences are great, 72% of customers will share them with other people. Lavish the same attention on your employees' experience as you do your customers if you want to make measurable progress on your societal value initiatives.

Let's step back in time to the period from 1960 to 1995 when the way companies related to consumers was mostly through their products as advertised on traditional media that encouraged us to buy them at the local store. Companies controlled the conversation, not customers. In the 1960s, consumers marveled at the conveniences of modern life, and companies worked hard to seem relatable through iconic characters, imagery, and promises of a happy home (with white families). The consumer experience was highly transactional, buying brands that gave us convenience and choice, in abundance. A company's social and environmental stances were not promoted, nor did they factor into purchase decisions, except for a minority of consumers. At the same time in the United States, the war in Vietnam, racial protests, political assassinations, and environmental pollution had shaken the national psyche. The first Earth Day event was held in April 1970 with 20 million people participating. Four months later, the Environmental Protection Agency (EPA) was formed. Those were pinnacle events. Environmental concerns declined afterward for the remainder of that decade. The 1980s brought a resurgence of environmental interest, partly as a response to Reagan administration policies, but waned again in the 1990s as consumers felt the financial pinch from growing environmental programs.[8] Since then evidence of environmental devastation has grown exponentially, climate events have accelerated in number and severity, economic inequality has worsened, several viral pandemics have hit, and social injustice worldwide has taken on justifiable urgency. The pace of consumption increased from the rise of the commercial internet from 1995 onward, and which goods are bought is poised for dramatic change again because consumers are paying attention to how your company behaves and whether it is good or bad for society, not just what products you sell.

Customers now control the conversation, not companies, so the sooner you deliver around the societal value motive, the better because it will be nearly impossible for your company to stop the snowball of negative customer feedback arising from poor ESG execution. Delivering on the societal value motive will be hard because of the difficulty of aligning the innumerable touchpoints (products, services, people, policies, marketing, supply chain, shareholders, facilities, etc.) that influence your stakeholder's experience. While more companies have taken important ESG-related steps, too many of these initiatives are "bolt on" temporary activities that are not viewed as core to the company's success. You must avoid this by shifting your force for good efforts from occasional to mission critical and by ensuring that the many dots that create the experiences your stakeholders have with your company are connected.

You may understandably wonder if focusing on creating great experiences will pay off. After all, you've already got superb products. The short answer is yes. Data show that relying on products alone to drive customer engagement won't sustain loyalty. Customers are far more aware of your company's efforts than mere product sales indicate, so you've got to be more than a logo with a slick marketing campaign. 59% of consumers globally (2019) are brand loyal because they perceive a personal connection, and in India more than 74% of consumers feel this way.[9] To deliver impactful sustainable value experiences requires a whole-company effort aimed at creating experiences that help people feel special and understood, such as surprising a supplier with public recognition during a company event for their sustainability contributions.

Consider Grundfos. You might not wake up each day wondering how the business of water pumps operates, especially as it relates to creating stakeholder experiences. Yet Grundfos, a Danish water pump manufacturer, has focused on customer-centric feedback since its founding in 1945. With more than 19,000 employees who produce over 16 million pumps and water solutions each year delivered to customers in over 80 countries, you can begin to understand the volume of customer touchpoints they track, now more than 200,000 *everyday* with digital technology. To manage this volume of feedback, Grundfos partnered with Qualtrics to implement a CX solution.

The data that are captured help Grundfos map every part of the customer's journey as they experience it. Their CX system alerts Grundfos' sales team, identifying the customer and situation. The insights help Grundfos work with frustrated customers quickly and directly to address their disappointment. And it is working, with customers rating Grundfos a 9 or higher on a 10 scale when evaluating their happiness. Furthermore, this success translated directly to a growth rate of happy customers more than 3x larger than unhappy customers.[10] Grundfos also started the Ghana Water Initiative to improve water access and positively impact daily life. The company has improved water access for over 60,000 people in Kenya, Vietnam, and Honduras. Their work helps address two of the UN's Sustainable Development Goals: SDG 6 – Clean Water and Sanitation, wherein by 2030 Grundfos will have helped improve safe drinking water access to 300 million people; SDG 13 – Climate Action, wherein by 2025 the company will have reduced their carbon emissions by 50%.[11]

Grundfos is a B2B example. Let's make the idea of experience more personal. Think of great experiences you have had where the sense of awe and exhilaration lifted you to another plane, making you feel and see the world differently. While the experience is temporary, the memory remains indelible. Perhaps it was that sense of joy you felt as a kid going to a live music event; or the rush you get when you hike the Mount Fitzroy trail in Argentina; or the wonder of "who even thinks of things like this?" when visiting Singapore's Supertrees. Experiences stimulate our senses and imaginations, but they don't have to be outsized spectacles to be meaningful. An experience tailored to a specific stakeholder can build the loyalty you are seeking.

Consider the world of travel. Traveling to another country can be an eye-opening experience. You will notice everything that is different from your own life experience. All of your senses are activated, absorbing the new stimuli. Things that run counter to how you understand them will cause you to wonder "why do they do it this way?" and give us a broader appreciation for how life has unfolded in different countries. Imagine if your next trip to another country also enabled you to contribute meaningfully to the community when you arrive by getting to know the people, developing relationships, and digging deeper to experience their world. Meet Givingway. Started in 2015, Givingway helps you, the traveler, immerse yourself in your chosen destination and have demonstrably positive impacts by volunteering to help while there. The locals, in turn, learn from you. It's called voluntourism and Givingway can do this because it has enlisted the support of more than 7,500 nonprofits in 144 countries. Givingway helps immerse us in the countries we visit in far more enriching ways and their model exemplifies how to create impactful experiences for stakeholders that go beyond the superficial. Givingway's model *awakens* the traveler's senses with its more immersive voluntourism experience; helps travelers *relate* to and connect with the people they are helping; and *cultivates* the traveler's curiosity by helping them experience daily life in depth.

Shaping experiences is important work and can have immensely impactful results. The ARC framework helps you design experiences from your stakeholder's point of view:

1. *Awaken* people's senses

2. *Relate* to people

3. *Cultivate* people's *curiosity*

## AWAKEN PEOPLE'S SENSES

If you've been to an EPL match, an Olympics, or any other major sports event, then you know that feeling of anticipation before the event begins. There is an indescribable euphoria that suspends disbelief and connects you to other fans and athletes in that shared moment. The event's unpredictability creates drama and tension and awakens a sense of expectation. Put yourself in your stakeholder's shoes. Ask "what would really create a 'wow' experience that ignites their senses and has them see us from a better and more sustainable perspective?" You probably don't know as that isn't a typical question to ask them, but we're not in typical times. Still, you might see this as a bridge too far if, for example, your company is a manufacturer of components for assembly line robots and you have defined success as cost efficiency arising from scale production (i.e., you are a commodity producer). However, deeper internal review might reveal that the components you make are a by-product of your in-house industrial design team's expertise and that their designs could also improve the equipment made by other companies in, for example, an EV (electric vehicles) ecosystem. By showing how your designs reduce systemic carbon emissions produced during the manufacturing process, you shift from being a commodity supplier to a preferred EV partner. Multiple wow experiences would be created: the enthusiastic endorsement from ecosystem partners who vouch for the quality of the components you produce and how you also created value for them; consumer appreciation for the end product they bought; shareholder delight from the improved financials resulting from multiple, sustainable revenue streams; and employee joy that they are the reason for the societal value created.

Awakening senses can begin by transparently describing your company's ESG investments, the corresponding impact on your operations, and the resulting measurable benefits to the markets you serve. Customers are paying attention to whether companies practice what they preach, so planning your communication will help them understand your sustainability efforts and even pre-empt any criticism that might otherwise arise in the absence of a clear understanding of your ESG investments. Plus, how your company demonstrates its ESG commitment, such as showing the measurable carbon emissions reductions in the example above, will help validate its reputation as a responsible societal actor and make it easier for customers to choose you over competitors. A survey (2018) of customers in the United Kingdom and United States found that 88% of respondents want brands to help them "be more environmentally friendly and ethical."[12] Consumers were asked for their views on sustainable apparel (2018) and 55% said they want to buy clothing considered "sustainable," although their understanding of "sustainability" varies. 48% were uncertain how to go about finding sustainable apparel. But in that same survey consumers expect companies to provide answers to their sustainability questions.[13]

Companies are not expected to shoulder the ESG burden alone as consumers do recognize the role they themselves play through the decisions they make. 96% of survey respondents (2018) believe their own actions can have a positive impact.[14] As the novel coronavirus pandemic escalated around the world in mid-2020, responsible people changed their behaviors knowing that their efforts could slow the virus's growth. Nearly 80% of consumers at that time said they would opt to make the same commitment to lifestyle changes to stop the climate crisis as they did in response to the pandemic, 57% were prepared to waste less, 50% would seek to avoid plastics, 40% were open to green energy alternatives, and qualitative findings showed that people believe that changing their behavior to improve the world is positive for society.[15]

## To Do

1. Ask your stakeholders what a "wow" experience is for them.

2. Ask your stakeholders what kind of "wow" experience would demonstrate sustainability and societal value.

3. Map out the internal operational requirements and external marketplace prototype initiatives needed to bring experiences to life.

## RELATE TO PEOPLE

An experience must feel personal to be effective. It must evoke a feeling that it was meant especially for that person, even though it may appeal to many. Early in my career I worked as sales director for the CEO of a five-star hotel company that had five hotels. I was 24 years old and quite inexperienced. The CEO invited me into his leadership team meeting and asked my opinion about a proposed marketing campaign. I recall the conflict I felt: I thought the campaign wasn't very good, but do I tell him and his team since one of them conceived of the idea? Or do I avoid offending and go along with it. I gulped and explained why I thought the campaign wasn't right. There was silence. Sweat beads formed on my forehead. Was I in trouble? Then the CEO asked me what I would do differently. He listened intently and when I was done, he smiled and agreed. My confidence soared. In that moment he made me believe my perspective mattered and that experience has influenced my work ever since. Relate to people by making them the center of your focus, whether 1:1 or through the way you orchestrate your company's touchpoints to create memorable experiences.

## To Do

1. Ask your stakeholder(s) what concerns them, what gives them hope, and what motivates them.

2. Ask your stakeholder(s) what makes your company relatable to them.

3. Ask your stakeholder(s) how your company can help them better.

## CULTIVATE PEOPLE'S CURIOSITY

Curiosity killed the cat. That's an idiom warning us of the risks of investigation. But curiosity didn't kill the cat, ignorance did. As children we asked "why" all the time, as questions helped us understand what we were experiencing, most of which was happening to us for the first time. As adults new experiences stimulate our curiosity and put our senses on high alert, and that curiosity precedes a sense of discovery, which is that moment when the unfamiliar becomes a revelation. Your desire to learn determines whether you retreat to the comfort of your opinions or grow from gaining new insight that challenges your assumptions. Being curious requires more from you than just finding ways to "satisfy stakeholder needs." Satisfaction is a boring term that conjures emotionless reactions, so stop using it. As I highlighted in Chapter 3, words matter so get people excited by using terms that express your transformation ambitions versus vocabulary that drains the energy from the room. The beauty of a great experience is that it opens our minds, heightens our curiosity, and inspires us to say "we have to do this more often." Your aim is to get your stakeholders to feel the same way. You are asking them to imagine things that don't yet exist, and their answers won't always be clear. But you will definitely gain useful insights when you take the time to carefully consider the descriptions you use and the curiosity you hope to inspire.

## To Do

1. Ask your stakeholder(s) what stimulates their curiosity (about anything).

2. Ask your stakeholder(s) their view of seeking input from others.

3. Ask your stakeholder(s) "what if" questions about how to fix a major problem (they define the problem).

## Quick Observations on Research

The ARC framework requires that you learn from your stakeholders what awakens their imagination, how you can relate to them, and what stimulates their curiosity. There are plenty of resources offering much deeper dives on robust research techniques. Absent clear internal direction businesses often use surveys hoping the insights will shed light on future direction. But the problem with some survey-based approaches is they can be backwards looking and tend to ask reactive questions lacking sharpness and precision, as opposed to more proactive inquiry focused on understanding how to demonstrably improve stakeholders' lives. You need to consciously break out of your typical survey questionnaire mindset by asking how you can gain fresh, meaningful insights. Doing it the same old way you've done it before will lead to the same old, tired, insights. Ethnographic and contextual research methods, used correctly, are powerful tools for learning about your stakeholders, are at the foundation of human-centered design, and are invaluable for revealing important insights stakeholders have about the kinds of experiences that would help them appreciate your societal value contributions. Much of my organizational work for the past 20 years has been in creating and teaching outcomes-driven executive education experiences with some terrific global educators. Companies didn't want knowledge "top-ups" or lectures on the latest academic research to develop their leaders. They wanted practical insights and tools they could use. We conducted extensive diagnostic and ethnographic research to understand the outcomes they sought, what they do well, and what frustrates them, using the findings to guide how we could help them.

## So What?

The ARC framework puts you in your stakeholder's shoes to create experiences that are meaningful to them. Creating great experiences isn't a luxury. It is table stakes required for entry into the larger need to become a force for good. Stakeholders have plenty of alternatives if you create sub-optimal experiences. Investors can easily shift to another company; customers can find another provider; value chain members can work with a different group of partners to accomplish their own ambitions; and employees won't tolerate for long a company that either pays lip service to contributing to society or conducts itself in a way that is demoralizing and toxic. What gets in the way of your company creating positive, meaningful, and impactful human experiences? Your current routines and structures. All of us are blinded to new approaches by the convenience of practices we have honed over many years. To break through these self-imposed barriers, do the following:

1. Identify what your stakeholder's current experience is truly like. Investigate by spending time with stakeholders directly, observing their behavior, and asking the penetrating questions that dig below the surface to understand what is important to them.
2. Identify the experience touchpoints from the stakeholder's perspective and be crystal-clear which ones you do well and which ones you need to fix. Then monitor the stakeholder's feedback.
3. Break down silos, structural blocks, and informal areas of impasse. Remember that you are not designing for your convenience, you are designing for the convenience of stakeholders.
4. Create a living document describing what the ideal human experience with your company should be. Ensure people internally understand this and invite their input, giving them agency to take on the responsibility for realizing this vision.

## End of Section 1

We've focused on identifying and developing *value meaning* for your company and how to support it. Remember, your aspiration is not to make money-that's a by-product of being clear on the meaningful value you intend to create. Here are summary questions to recap the main themes:

1. Why are we here?
    (a) Identify the meta-challenge and the problem you are solving within.
    (b) Identify why you are uniquely qualified to help solve this.
    (c) Identify the capabilities you need to make it happen.
    (d) Identify the ways people's experiences will change because of what your company does.

In the next section we'll focus on Value Measure by explaining four value dimensions that will help your company succeed with its force for good transformation.

## NOTES

1. Keats, J., & Forman, H. B. (1895). The letters of John Keats. P.305. Retrieved from https://books.google.com/books?hl=en&lr=&id=cDMOAAAAYAAJ&oi=fnd&pg=PR13&dq=nothing+ever+becomes+real+until+it+is+experienced+John+keats&ots=kQFIwfCYJ7&sig=NCtqoVSxF2dXIx4agfh9bpA96Pk#v=onepage&q=nothing%20ever%20becomes%20real%20until%20it%20is%20experienced%20John%20keats&f=false.
2. De Luce, I. (2019). Something profound happens when astronauts see Earth from space for the first time. Insider. Retrieved from https://www.businessinsider.com/overview-effect-nasa-apollo8-perspective-awareness-space-2015-8.
3. No author. (2020). Experience is everything. Get it right. PwC 2020 Consumer Survey. Retrieved from https://www.pwc.com/us/en/services/consulting/library/consumer-intelligence-series/future-of-customer-experience.html.
4. Mosher, A., Norwood, J., Tonk, L., Webb, G., & Turner, R. (2021). Transforming employee experience: A SWOT analysis of 500 human resources departments. Isolved. Retrieved from https://www.isolvedhcm.com/assets/isolved_HR_Leader_Report.pdf.
5. Sethi, B., Lamm, J., & Caglar, D. (2021). Your post-pandemic business: How to keep your business moving and emerge stronger. PwC. Retrieved from https://www.pwc.com/us/en/services/consulting/workforce-of-the-future/library/post-pandemic-workforce-considerations.html.
6. Burrell, L. Co-creating employee experience. Harvard Business Review. (2018). Retrieved from https://www.hbsp.harvard.edu/product/S18022-PDF-ENG?Ntt=co-creating%20the%20employee%20experience.
7. Gilbert, J. (2019). The direct connection between employee experience and customer experience (and how to improve both). Forbes. Retrieved from https://www.forbes.com/sites/forbescommunicationscouncil/2019/09/04/the-direct-connection-between-employee-experience-and-customer-experience-and-how-to-improve-both/?sh=5c4f3d25f608.
8. Pulia, M. (2008). Public opinion on environmental issues: does it influence government action? Res Publica – Journal of Undergraduate Research. 6(1), Article 8. P.3. Retrieved from https://digitalcommons.iwu.edu/cgi/viewcontent.cgi?referer=https://www.google.com/&httpsredir=1&article=1082&context=respublica.
9. Authors: KPMG consumer & retail team. (2019). The truth about consumer loyalty. KMPG. P.4. Retrieved from https://assets.kpmg/content/dam/kpmg/ar/pdf/the-truth-about-customer-loyalty.pdf.

10. Multiple sources: (1) No author. (2021). XM Blog. 6 world-class B2B CX examples to learn from. Qualtrics. Retrieved from https://www.qualtrics.com/blog/b2b-cx-examples/. (2) No author. (2019). B2B marketing. discover how Grundfos keeps its pulse on 200,000 daily customer interactions. Retrieved from https://www.b2bmarketing.net/en/resources/articles/discover-how-grundfos-keeps-its-pulse-200000-daily-customer-interactions.
11. No author. (2021). Grundfos sustainability report. Retrieved from https://www.grundfos.com/about-us/news-and-media/reports/sustainability-report-2020.
12. Townsend, S. (2018). 88% of consumers want you to help them make a difference. Forbes. Retrieved from https://www.forbes.com/sites/solitairetownsend/2018/11/21/consumers-want-you-to-help-them-make-a-difference/?sh=3775693c6954.
13. Clark, S. (2021). 4 ways sustainability affects the customer experience. CMS Wire. Retrieved from https://www.cmswire.com/customer-experience/4-ways-sustainability-affects-the-customer-experience/.
14. Townsend, S. (2018). 88% of consumers want you to help them make a difference. Forbes. Retrieved from https://www.forbes.com/sites/solitairetownsend/2018/11/21/consumers-want-you-to-help-them-make-a-difference/?sh=3775693c6954.
15. Townsend, S. (2020). Near 80% of people would personally do as much for climate as they have for coronavirus. Forbes. Retrieved from https://www.forbes.com/sites/solitairetownsend/2020/06/01/near-80-of-people-would-personally-do-as-much-for-climate-as-they-have-for-coronavirus/.

# Section 2

# VALUE MEASURE

# 5

# STRENGTHENING REPUTATIONAL VALUE

*Glass, China, and Reputation, are easily crack'd, and never well mended.*[1]

*—Benjamin Franklin*

"How do we make sure that Boards of Directors are making informed decisions?" This question animates Helle Bank Jørgensen work as Founder and CEO of Competent Boards, which she started in 2019, and is the culmination of her decades of work at the forefront of sustainability, ESG, climate, and corporate responsibility. A company's ability to credibly impact society positively depends on its reputation which, in turn, depends on the actions of its Board, CEO, employees, and value chain partners. Helle brings a wealth of knowledge into her work with company boards as more of them embrace sustainability as a strategic imperative for their companies and the strengthening of their reputations as a by-product. She created the world's first Green Account, the world's first Integrated Report (that shows the connection across business operations, supply chains, and environmental impact), and was the principal organizer for the CEO and Investor Network on Business Ethics and Nonfinancial Reporting. She developed the first integrated supply chain for IKEA and she worked with Nike on how to embed sustainability into their business functions. She was recognized in 2019 with the Clean50 award.[2] Throughout her work Helle has seen where company sustainability efforts succeed or fail. Success happens when sustainability is embedded deep into a company's operations and processes and not simply treated as a project. Over the years she has cultivated meaningful relationships with leading CEOs and Boards, understands their issues, and helps them become proponents for sustainability issues. The timing of her work is more important than ever because the actions of our companies set a precedent, and the more that organizations act sustainably, the better the outcomes for businesses everywhere, for society, and for the environment.[3]

The UN's IPCC 2021 report was described as "code red for humanity" by the UN Secretary General, António Guterres. The report's findings were the most detailed ever, citing the role of humankind in warming the planet and worsening the climate crisis. Earth's surface temperatures have risen faster the past 50 years than at any other similar period over the last 2,000 years, with a 1.1°C increase since 1850. If the current trends continue then the next 20 years are projected to see a 1.5°C or more increase, which would be catastrophic if we do not act now to stop destructive practices.[4] This is where any company, supported by its board, must play a direct and proactive role by developing the practices, process changes, and innovations to help address the climate crisis, and improving its understanding about ESG, beyond surface knowledge. According to the Sustainability Board Report, 63 of the top 100 global companies have board committees dedicated to sustainability. That is encouraging, but we need more companies doing this. Furthermore, only 17% of those sustainability committee board members have actual ESG expertise.[5] Helle's Competent Boards fills this vital need for board members: gaining fluency in sustainability issues that is just as robust as their fluency in financial matters, helping them more effectively advocate for doing what is right for society.

Running a company is no easy undertaking. As a leader you must ensure the viability of the business as measured by financial growth while also ensuring all employees perform their work in an aligned manner, supporting your company's strategic aspiration. When your company performs well, it builds trust that impacts your reputation positively. In a world animated by converging crises, where climate change, social injustice, economic inequality, and pandemics affect how we work and live, the role of your company today has never been more important. You want to know that you have earned trust by being a steward of societal value.

Edelman's Trust Barometer (2021), a global study measuring trust in governments, media, business, and NGOs, focused on two dimensions: competences and ethics. The only institution that was seen as both competent and ethical was business, barely scoring in the positive on ethics. NGOs were viewed as ethical but not competent. Government was seen negatively on both dimensions, as was media. Businesses and their leaders have a real opportunity to improve on both dimensions and aspiring to be a force for good is the guiding star illuminating the path. There are dozens of touchpoints that influence any company's reputation, but in my work the following three areas consistently determine reputation quality:

- Strong ethical and moral compass

- Transparency

- Market perceptions

## STRONG ETHICAL AND MORAL COMPASS

In 2018 David Hogg was a senior student at Stoneman Douglas High School in Parkland, Florida when a mass shooting killed 17 of his classmates and injured another 17. It was a brutal, devastating, and senseless act that ended the lives of young students with otherwise bright futures, an all-too-common occurrence in the United States. The victims' families confronted an unimaginable nightmare, and the outpouring of support and grief nationwide was palpable. Surviving classmates knew their lives would never be the same. They channelled their energy into a series of gun control rallies around the United States. When tragedy strikes, whether it is a mass shooting or destructive hurricane or deadly epidemic, one would expect people to set aside differences to support others in their time of need. Laura Ingraham, a TV host on Fox News in the United States, reacted differently. A few weeks after the Parkland massacre she mocked Hogg on Twitter for college rejections he had received. She was roundly criticized.[6] In response Hogg did not attack her but went after her advertisers instead, asking them to pull their ads from her show. His campaign was a success, she lost nearly two dozen advertisers, and Ingraham later apologized, but the commercial damage was done. The advertiser boycotts were a visible public rebuke of Ingraham's thoughtless tweet. One advertiser, Wayfair – a global company that sells home goods online, said "The decision of an adult to personally criticize a high school student who has lost his classmates in an unspeakable tragedy is not consistent with our values."[7] It took the loss of commercial revenues to get Ingraham to apologize and as advertisers have suggested, questionable ethics and morality are why many advertisers boycotted her show.

In Chapter 1, I introduced you to Ravi Kumar's work at Infosys providing reskilling and upskilling education opportunities in the United States. Infosys was recognized by Ethisphere as among the world's most ethical companies and one of only four in the Global Software and Services industry. Infosys was selected for its integrity and values-based decision-making, and the company's efforts in workforce education, including its goal of helping 10 million people attain digital skills by 2025. Ravi's perspective is refreshingly progressive and demonstrates Infosys' values. Business as a force for good while also being financially successful are not incompatible pursuits, they go hand in hand. As Ravi said, "Societal impact *is* good business. You cannot achieve your vision or mission without understanding how to improve the ecosystem around you. Part of my work is influencing people everywhere to realize that they will be disrupted if they *don't* help contribute to making society better." Infosys's annual ESG report (Infosys ESG 2021) offers an encouraging summary of their ongoing efforts[8]:

Environment
- Became carbon neutral in 2021, 30 years ahead of the Paris Agreement deadline of 2050.

- 50% of electricity in the company's India operations is renewable

Social
- Multiple awards and industry recognition as one of the world's best places to work (Top Employers Global Certification; Great Place to Work®)

- 38.6% women in workforce

- Infosys's Reskill and Restart program, launched in July 2020, has already created 560 courses in 18 career streams to help American workers prepare for a more digital future

Governance
- 22% women on Board

- 71% of spend is local to India

- 248 suppliers recognized as having a significant social and environmental impact

## TRANSPARENCY

Transparency is a requirement at both the institutional and individual levels. Your company's reputation for being open and honest with stakeholders will determine whether it is trusted. Generational differences may influence a person's willingness to be transparent. In the cybersecurity sector employees under the age of 30 are five times more likely to acknowledge failure, whereas only 10% of those over age 51 are willing to do so.[9] Openly admitting one's professional mistakes and gaffes is difficult for many people, but research by Alison Wood Brooks (2018) shows that such openness reduces the incidence of malicious envy, a toxic impulse people have to tear down another person's success.[10] When Jim Whitehurst was CEO of Red Hat, an open source technology company, he admitted a major mistake soon after acquiring a company that wasn't fully open source. Rather than rewrite the acquiree's code, he decided to go to market as is. The response was overwhelmingly negative. He apologized, had the code rewritten, and went to market a year late. Whitehurst took responsibility and explained how he had made these decisions, which was appreciated by employees and customers. His forthright actions prevented long-term trust erosion.[11]

What we've learned, especially in the past 25 years of technology advances, is that people appreciate it greatly when the company where they work promotes transparency in a way that makes people feel like they are trusted, heard, understood and that the business is fundamentally trying to do well by doing good. Edelman's Trust Barometer (2021) shows that 56% of people in society at large worry that business leaders knowingly mislead (and 57% are concerned that government leaders do the same).[12] This should worry you, even if your company has a trusted reputation, because the broader perception of business could lead to guilt by association. Research by Robert Half® (2020) found that 82% of employees want their employers to share financial updates. Their findings also show that 68% of public companies and 55% of private firms share financial updates with employees.[13]

Given the gap between what employees want and what companies do, there is an opportunity for you to improve transparency. However, transparency does not mean all data and conversations are public. There are inevitably sensitive topics to be considered from both the outward-facing (your company's contribution to society) and inward-facing (showing people how their work connects to the company's distinctive aspiration) perspectives.

## Outward

Your company's transparency ultimately finds its way into reputation rankings from trusted sources (RepTrak™, Edelman Trust Barometer, GreatPlacetoWork®...). You can influence your company's reputation by paying attention to several levers:

- Board of Directors' familiarity with and support for key issues like sustainability, as Helle Bank Jørgensen's Competent Boards helps provide.

- Performance guidance for shareholders of public companies.

- Your consistent, open sharing with ecosystem partners.

- Keeping industry/technology analysts updated on your company's business advances helps them gauge the health of your sector.

- Being active in all customer forums. Active online, digital, and mobile efforts to resolve customer needs show the market that you are paying attention.

A study of companies in the food industry (2016) found that 73% of people will pay *more* for a product that promises total transparency, 39% said they would change to a brand that was focused on transparency, and 81% said they were open to trying a company's entire suite of products if they had trust in its transparency.[14] Similar results are found in other sectors. Consumers are often ahead of companies in their expectations of what defines a successful product, a consequence of companies delivering *after* consumer needs have been articulated, whereas consumers are shaping where they want things to go and expect companies to do good by doing right, whether that is supporting sustainability, social injustice, or economic inequality. In a study of European consumers (2020)[15]

- 88% want companies to reduce pollution

- 57% have made significant lifestyle changes because of Covid-19

- 60% are making additional effort to recycle and to buy responsible products

- 67% believe use of sustainable materials is among their buying criteria

A banking survey (2021) found the following reaction from consumers if they discovered their bank had committed a FDIC/government violation[16]

- 66% of Baby Boomers would leave

- 44% of Gen Z would leave

- 46% of Millennials would leave

- 58% of Gen X would leave

Crises reveal whether our companies are compassionate about people. Vancity is a Canadian credit union with a reputation in its communities as a financial institution that cares about people. With jobs being lost, small business revenues reduced to close to zero, and simple life experiences like vacation travel suspended, Vancity focused on helping its local communities stay afloat during the height of the pandemic.

- For small business they offered zero interest working capital loans.

- For individual customers they reduced credit card rates to zero and waived ATM fees.

- They bought foreign currencies back from customers whose trips were canceled, at full value.

- They launched a $1 million community response fund to support local groups.

- They helped create a Unity Term Deposit to support people directly impacted by Covid-19, raising $200 million in 30 days.

## Inward

How you treat employees also finds its way into the societal milieu. Pay attention to key data as well as the social pulse inside your organization:

- Internal demographics (diversity, equity, and inclusion)

- Financial and workplace performance (are you achieving financial success but creating a toxic culture?)

- Whether your company's actions are aligned with its values

Employee compensation practices influence individual perceptions. But note that pay transparency is tricky. A LinkedIn survey (2019) showed that 27% of HR organizations shared salary ranges within roles with candidates and another 22% expect to do this in the next few years. 51% of those surveyed said that pay ranges were mysterious.[17] McKinsey reported that pay transparency comes with risks. Supporters advocate employees should be treated as adults and trusted accordingly whereas detractors point out that many employees lack the full context about how pay is determined and can create false narratives that undermine the reasons for transparency in the first place.[18] If your company has known pay discrepancies, then the socially responsible response is for you to fix those now. There are few things that can sink a company faster than internal rebellion over unfair pay practices, and the reputational harm takes a long time to repair if left unchecked.

Your company's healthcare benefits are another contributor to your reputation. Healthcare is a basic human need and despite the political debate in some countries, especially the United States, creating positive societal value means a billionaire is no more deserving of quality care than an economically disadvantaged person (the challenges in the United States are exacerbated by a flawed healthcare system that, as Dr BJ Miller (2015) states, is designed around diseases not people.)[19] This opens the door of opportunity for healthcare providers, both start-up and established, to redefine how to provide basic care, build their reputations, and enhance the reputations of companies that subscribe to their services. Covid-19 accelerated the need for innovative healthcare solutions because it forced many people to rely on telemedicine services. Aging populations in developed countries are fueling growth as well. According to VentureBeat (2021) healthcare start-ups globally raised $80.6 billion in 2020 across 5,523 deals, showing substantial growth over 2019's $53.7 billion (5,450 deals). In 2016 total investment was $34.4 billion for 4,140 deals.[20] To illustrate, look at Ro, a healthcare technology company founded in 2017 with the expressed purpose of being a patient-centric provider, not disease-centric. Ro also provides healthcare access to "care deserts," sparsely populated areas where people do not have easy access to proper care. Ro's platform allows working professionals to access care beyond traditional business hours, saving people the hassle of taking time off and/or arranging for child/adult care. Since its launch the company has quickly built an ecosystem comprising in-home care, diagnostics, health providers, and pharmacy partners. Patients pay with cash because Ro does not accept insurance. As of mid-2021 Ro had supported more than 6 million digital healthcare visits comprising 46 million patient touchpoints, reach 98% of care deserts in the United States. Ro assures patients of no-surprises transparency, so they receive prices and sourcing information for medications before deciding.[21] The benefits of Ro's design (and of many other new telemedicine healthcare providers) are less wait time, cheaper medical costs (depending on the condition), elimination of insurance-related logistical hassles, and better access for those in remote areas.

Poor transparency can harm people's trust and overall organizational effectiveness. Work with your teams to discuss the following:

1. What do we intend to gain by improving transparency?

2. What is sensitive information that should be walled off from broader consumption?

3. What parameters govern the sharing of individual performance evaluations?

4. What is needed to enable teams of people to share and collaborate effectively?

5. What time limits should we place on information access linked to specific projects?

6. How will we handle problems arising from transparency revelations?

7. What do we define as explicit violation of transparency guidelines?

It is surprising how many well-intentioned people and companies still slip up and breach ethical and moral norms. Most people intellectually understand and are capable of making sound moral and ethical choices, but actions sometimes belie understanding. Ask the following to ensure the right conduct is encouraged, rewarded, and lived.

1. Are your company values explicitly known by all employees and nonemployee stakeholders?

2. Are your company values integrated into your hiring and development?

3. Are ethics and morality embedded in employee performance evaluations?

4. What challenges has your company faced in the past that could have led to a moral or ethical breach?

## MARKET PERCEPTIONS

Market perceptions are notoriously difficult to manage, particularly if your company is saying one thing while doing something contrary. The public will quickly pick up on such transgressions of trust and rake your company over the proverbial hot coals of societal disdain. Market perceptions begin with your CEO, under the Board's guidance, because leading by example is critical to influencing others and creating credible impact. SJR, a corporate communications company, conducted a 2020 analysis of perception of U.S. corporate CEOs during the early months of the Covid-19 crisis using publicly available data from articles and different social media posts about them.[22] More than 6 million social media were analyzed. SJR's logic was that the social conversation in the ether was a good barometer of what people were discussing about how, where, and when CEOs were communicating about the pandemic. Importantly, the volume of media interviews was not what distinguished the top CEOs. Instead, the best CEOs were focused on frequently engaging with key stakeholder groups, notably customers, employees, and partners. In addition, 56% of the top 25 CEOs regularly posted something human and emotional in their LinkedIn entries, whereas only 33% of the bottom 75 CEOs did this.[23]

How you lead your company to become a credible force for good will be a core differentiator distinguishing tomorrow's successful companies from those that fail to adapt to today's challenges. There is a caution: a lofty market perception will fall quickly if the public detects BS and/or disingenuousness. A 2018 study by The Economist of the eight largest business scandals in recent years found a value decrease of approximately 30% from what firms otherwise would have been valued if they had not been subjected to scandal.[24] Therefore, your trust-building efforts need to include proactively countering any potential distrust among your stakeholders. 78% of consumers with high brand trust will recommend a company to others and say they're willing to "defend the brand against criticism" if they trust it, yet that trust is quickly eroded if your company abuses its relationship with stakeholders.[25]

Data abuse is a particularly notable example. With social media firms like Facebook tracking what people do as they navigate the internet, privacy concerns are understandably growing (the 2020 US Presidential election shed light on the algorithms used to target ads, and misinformation, based on our social media interests). Europe's GDPR (General Data Protection Regulation), implemented in 2018, created a higher standard for protecting a person's personal information for other countries to follow. Even with such regulation, data abuse remains a concern, especially as the volume of hacking increases. Having a perfect global standard that protects everyone is unlikely for many years, so the onus is on companies to strengthen their data protection standards and IT systems to reduce the chances of consumer data being misused. Research by Pew in the United States revealed that 79% of Americans had concern about how companies use the data collected about them, 81% are concerned that the risks of the data collected about them outweigh the benefits, and 64% have seen ads based on using their personal data.[26] Edelman research found analogous results, with 70% of consumers polled saying they use at least one, if not more, advertising avoidance methods.[27] Building trust with consumers and other key stakeholders helps convert them into advocates. In effect, they act as influencers. Influencers play a vital role because the trust they engender among other people encourages them to follow the influencer's recommendations. 63% of consumers trust influencers more than a company's advertising.[28] And they trust actions. A

2020 RepTrak™ survey showed that most industries and companies within improved their reputations during the pandemic because of the care they showed for their own employees and because of the visibility their support for social movements received. Pharmaceuticals, Food and Beverage, and Transport were the three sectors that had the strongest reputation gains. The public noticed and gave their thumbs up. The biggest declines in reputation? Airlines, hospitality, and government.[29] Part of the US government's reputation decline in 2020 was due to the Trump Administration's poor handling of the Covid-19 pandemic.[30]

## SO WHAT?

In decades past, being financially successful and having a respected brand were both critical for gaining credibility with markets and customers. That has changed. Having a strong ethical and moral compass and being transparent drive modern market perceptions and affect company reputations, and we ignore these at our peril. The tone set at the top about your company's seriousness to be more sustainable, from the Board and CEO, has a significant impact on your company's reputation. While this is hard work, we know this will pay off: 81% of sustainable indexes in 2020 performed better than "their parent benchmarks."[31] More than 60% of consumers (2016) believe in the importance of buying from companies that are sustainable, better for the environment, and helpful to society. A reputation for corporate responsibility can improve price premiums and revenues by 20% and also improve a company's attractiveness to employees while strengthening the company's culture.[32] Right now is an ideal time to become a force for good and bolster your company's reputation. In Chapter 6, we'll dive into the importance of harnessing organization value.

## NOTES

1. The Franklin Institute. (1750). Benjamin Franklin's famous quotes. Retrieved from https://www.fi.edu/benjamin-franklin/famous-quotes.
2. No author. (2019). The clean50 2019. Retrieved from https://clean50.com/honourees/?award=clean50&year=2019&cat=&s=.
3. Based on 2021 author Interviews with Helle Bank Jørgensen.

4. 234 authors from 66 countries. (2021). Intergovernmental Panel on Climate Change (IPCC) report. Retrieved from https://www.ipcc.ch/2021/08/09/ar6-wg1-20210809-pr/.

5. Five contributing authors (p. 14). (2020). The sustainability board report 2021 (pp. 2–3). Retrieved from https://a89c8240-f3c4-4e8b-b920-fae532-b127b6.filesusr.com/ugd/f6724f_dd6a0102c0164d97bff1cfa4abf74583.pdf.

6. Multiple sources: (1) Victor, D. (2018). Advertisers drop Laura Ingraham after she taunts parkland survivor David Hogg. The New York Times. Retrieved from https://www.nytimes.com/2018/03/29/business/media/laura-ingraham-david-hogg.html; (2) Hod, I. (2018). Mitsubishi drops Laura Ingraham as advertiser boycott campaign continues (Exclusive). The wrap. Retrieved from https://www.thewrap.com/mitsubishi-becomes-24th-company-to-drop-laura-ingraham-exclusive/.

7. See footnote 6.

8. Multiple sources: (1) Interviews with Ravi Kumar, President of Infosys (2021); (2) Infosys ESG report (2021). (p. 9). Retrieved from https://www.infosys.com/about/corporate-responsibility/sustainability-reports.html.

9. Truta, F. (2020). Companies should tell workers it's ok to confess to security mistakes, Stanford professor says. BitDefender. Retrieved from https://businessinsights.bitdefender.com/workers-confess-security-mistakes-stanford-professor.

10. Gerdeman, D. (2018). Harvard business school working knowledge. Retrieved from https://hbswk.hbs.edu/item/why-managers-should-publicize-their-failures.

11. Whitehurst, J. (2015). Being a leader means admitting mistakes. Boston Globe. Retrieved from https://www.bostonglobe.com/business/2015/07/03/being-leader-means-admittng-mistakes/X1xynMqmKpKCiAhv4CRngP/story.html.

12. No author. (2021). Edelman trust barometer team. Edelman trust barometer 2021 global report. (p. 21). Retrieved from https://www.edelman.com/sites/g/files/aatuss191/files/2021-01/2021-edelman-trust-barometer.pdf.

13. Ahuja, S. (2020). Survey: 82% of workers want updates on company financial performance. Robert Half Management Resources. Retrieved from https://rh-us.mediaroom.com/2020-01-28-Survey-82-Of-Workers-Want-Updates-On-Company-Financial-Performance.

14. Kline, K. (2016). Here's how important brand transparency is for your business. Inc. From a Study by Label Insight entitled 2016 Label Insight Transparency ROI Study. Retrieved from https://www.inc.com/kenny-kline/new-study-reveals-just-how-important-brand-transparency-really-is.html.

15. Granskog, A., Lee, L., Sawyers, C., & Magnus, K.- H. (2020). Survey: Consumer sentiment on sustainability in fashion. McKinsey. Retrieved from https://www.mckinsey.com/industries/retail/our-insights/survey-consumer-sentiment-on-sustainability-in-fashion.

16. No author (2021). New crisis survey reveals younger generations more concerned about social issues at their bank than boomers. York Public Relations. Retrieved from https://www.yorkpublicrelations.com/press-room/new-crisis-survey-reveals-younger-generations-more-concerned-about-social-issues-at-their-bank-than-boomers/.

17. McLaren, S. (2019). Why these 3 companies are sharing how much their employees make. *LinkedIn Talent Blog*. Retrieved from https://www.linkedin.com/business/talent/blog/talent-strategy/why-these-companies-are-sharing-how-much-employees-make.

18. Birkinshaw, J., & Cable, D. (2017). The dark side of transparency. *McKinsey Quarterly*. Retrieved from https://www.mckinsey.com/business-functions/organization/our-insights/the-dark-side-of-transparency.

19. Miller, B. J. (2015). What really matters at the end of life. TED.com. Retrieved from: https://www.ted.com/talks/bj_miller_what_really_matters_at_the_end_of_life.

20. O'Brien, C. (2021). Pandemic drove VC funding for healthcare to record $80.6 billion in 2020. Venture Beat. Retrieved from: https://venturebeat.com/2021/01/20/pandemic-drove-vc-funding-for-health-care-to-record-80-6-billion-in-2020/.

21. Ro. The patient company (2021). Retrieved from: https://ro.co.

22. No author (2020). The CEO leaderboard: Covid-19 reputation rankings. SJR-A WPP Company. Retrieved from https://www.groupsjr.com/ceoleaderboard/.

23. See footnote 22.

24. Ryder, B. (2018). Getting a handle on a scandal. *The Economist*. Retrieved from https://www.economist.com/business/2018/03/28/getting-a-handle-on-a-scandal.

25. See footnote 24.

26. Auxier, B., Rainie, L., Anderson, M., Perrin, A., Kumar, M., & Turner, E. (2019). Americans and privacy: Concerned, confused and feeling lack of control over their personal information. Pew Research Center. Retrieved from https://www.pewresearch.org/internet/2019/11/15/americans-and-privacy-concerned-confused-and-feeling-lack-of-control-over-their-personal-information/.

27. No author (2020). Edelman intelligence. Trust barometer special report: Brand trust in 2020. Retrieved from https://www.edelman.com/research/brand-trust-2020.

28. Grieb, S., Newland, A., & Po, M. (2019). The power of influencers. Edelman. Retrieved from https://www.edelman.com/research/the-power-of-influencers.

29. Lambert, L. In corporate America we trust? (2021). Despite perennial crisis, business reputations are rising. *Fortune*. Retrieved from https://fortune.com/2021/01/14/corporate-america-business-reputation-survey/.

30. Wike, R., Fetterolf, J. & Mordecai, M. (2020). US image plummets internationally as most say country has handled coronavirus badly. Pew Research Center. Retrieved from https://www.pewresearch.org/global/2020/09/15/us-image-plummets-internationally-as-most-say-country-has-handled-coronavirus-badly/.
31. No author (2021). The ESG moral compass. World Finance. Retrieved from https://www.worldfinance.com/special-reports/esg-a-moral-compass-for-business.
32. Whelan, T., & Fink, C. (2016). The comprehensive case for sustainability. Harvard Business Review, pp. 7–8. Retrieved from https://www.hbsp.harvard.edu/product/H037U0-PDF-ENG?Ntt5The%20Comprehensive%20Business%20Case%20for%20Sustainability.

# 6

# INSPIRING ORGANIZATIONAL VALUE

*The best way to find yourself is to lose yourself in the service of others.*[1]

–*Mahatma Gandhi*

Anthony Guerrero grew up in a poor community, but there was something about the spirit of the place that he loved. By age 10 he was pretty darn good at his job. He had an early morning paper route, he knew his customers (and they knew him), and he had developed a technique for flinging the papers from his bike so that they would skip once then land on the porch. He didn't miss. As his skill grew, so did his confidence, and his desire to find ways to be more effective at his job. He enlisted his dad, mom, and sister. His mom and sister rolled the papers and his dad helped collect the money. He did this not because he didn't want to do the work but because the more efficient he was, the more he could recruit additional customers, and the more time he could spend with his friends after his route was done for the day. At the ripe old age of 10 he had built a collaborative system, with the right people in the right places helping to get work done. His customers loved his entrepreneurial spirit and he loved being a trusted part of his community's daily routine. His connection to community went beyond his paper route. After school he played baseball as often as he could for as long as he could. He was with his friends playing with other friends on neighboring teams. The game would stop, even in the middle of a play, when the local burrito food truck drove up. Kids from both teams would run to the truck. The owner gave them all free burritos that were "so warm and so good," contributing to a sense of community camaraderie. The game was forgotten. The generosity of that burrito truck owner no doubt affected his profits since they had their own ecosystem of suppliers to pay. But profitability wasn't the point. Societal value was. Talking to Anthony today (he is Chairman of the International Future Living Institute and Vice President of Workplace Strategies and Real Estate at Earth Justice) you can't help but smile as he shares his childhood stories. His family, his friends and the burrito truck driver all demonstrated a generosity of spirit that united everyone. That same spirit permeates his work to this day, and it exemplifies the qualities of the best performing companies that generate organizational value.[2]

Anthony's stories convey the uplifting spirit from people on a team who have shared interests and values. We know what it is like to be on a talented sports team, or to be part of an operation considered a well-oiled machine, or to feel like your organization is doing something incredibly special. A sense of cause is best fostered when the objective being pursued feels special, not incidental, or incremental. Radically transforming to a more responsible approach to business that positively impacts society creates a special call to action that inspires people to rally around it.

I introduced Janice Lao to you in Chapter 2. Her cross-disciplinary skills as an Environmental Scientist and Development Economist have influenced the ESG policies everywhere she has worked. She has focused on getting boards, senior management, and employees to adopt a sustainability mindset and corresponding practices. Janice says her role is not to narrowly prescribe specs as that reduces flexibility. The scientific evidence is clear. Facts are facts. Rather than commanding people to act responsibly because the data says you must, she invites them to join a workplace community pursuing sustainability. She says doing this is a bit of a dance to find what inspires others to help build a movement. As more people participate the lighter the load per person, a lesson that is not lost on her, or others, as they work to achieve their ESG ambitions. Janice tailors her appeals to each unique audience-her bosses, the board, and employees-helping them see where they fit into the sustainability "dance," and she always thanks people for trusting her. Janice epitomizes the saying "If you want to go quickly, go alone. If you want to go far, go together."

It's easy to say no to anything that upsets our comfortable routines. Why rock the boat? Plus, company cultures are complex, so where do you begin the change effort? Yet most of us know that electric sensation of working with others to accomplish something important. When it succeeds, it feels great (just think about those victories you had in sports). When it fails, it doesn't feel great, but you then channel your team energies toward improving before the next opportunity. There are certainly times when working together fails miserably and team members vow never to work collaboratively in that particular configuration again, but even such a sour experience reveals lessons that, when shared, help improve the next team effort.

Organizational value is enhanced multiple ways, but we'll focus on three key areas as these are the most pertinent to your company:

1. Employees: do people feel like their work matters and that what they are doing is connected to a larger cause?

2. Market: do investors and customers believe that the company is guided by trustworthy leaders who are interested in the greater good?

3. Ecosystem: do value chain partners believe that the host organization honors its commitments and supports the entire chain of interdependent relationships as opposed to being a cudgel that demands conformity at all costs?

## EMPLOYEES

Harvard's John Kotter et al. (2008) described how organization value is created through employees. Their findings should give CEOs and business leaders the confidence to make culture transformation a priority. According to Kotter, companies with adaptable cultures saw their revenues grow four times faster than those lacking an adaptable culture; job creation was over seven times higher; stock prices grew 12 times faster, profits were 750% higher, new revenues grew 700%, and customer satisfaction levels doubled.[3] You may have experienced the kind of positive conditions that reward impactful work, even if it failed. Now provide that same encouragement to your employees. What is surprising is how difficult it is for companies to make organizational value creation a priority. A common refrain from many of the leaders I've worked with is that the people stuff is the hard stuff. As one CEO pointed out, he took greater comfort in analyzing spreadsheets because those use basic, predictable methods for analytical problem-solving, whereas the methods for solving people issues are unpredictable and idiosyncratic, and lack the satisfying "data in, answer out" that formulas provide. Another told me that people issues remind her of a black hole; once you get sucked in, you never get out.

I've been involved in several turnarounds and acquisitions, ranging from helping struggling business units within large companies, to revamping higher education curricula to adapt to market and societal needs, to start-ups seeking to reposition themselves after early market forays struggled. I've seen people in tough times confront a range of emotions and stresses that can feel very isolating, compounding their doubts and anxiety. While each company faces difficult circumstances at times, you must help employees regain confidence and forestall turning a challenge into a disaster. True organization value is realized when employees gain a sense of hope, contribution, and agency:

*Hope:* When work feels like a special cause and that your company's aspiration is fulfilling important societal needs, it gives people a sense of hope. Provide psychological protection for your employees while the company navigates the choppy waters. Employees will push through challenges if they believe that their leaders are looking out for the entire organization. Give regular updates about how the business is doing, what adjustments are needed, and how decisions being made will affect their respective areas as doing so will help foster esprit de corps. A Bain study (2020) found that 75% of employees worldwide were proud of how their companies supported them as COVID-19 unfolded, and 64% felt a similar pride in how their company looked after the interests of the overall community.[4] Jacqueline Mattis, Dean of Faculty at Rutgers University, encourages the following five strategies (paraphrased) for encouraging hope[5]:

1. Establish goals: hopeful people "imagine and act." Create conditions in your company that encourage employees to set goals and a plan for achieving them.

2. Leverage uncertainty: uncertainty means that many options likely exist, so start identifying and testing them.

3. Notice what you're noticing: avoid bombarding yourself with negative stimuli that only serve to reinforce trying conditions.

4. Connect to Community: when we're alone we can fall into the rabbit hole of our own doubt. Connecting with family, friends and colleagues refreshes us by helping us hear and see different perspectives.

5. Evidence matters: don't rely just on opinion or beliefs, rely on data as it helps us track our efforts.

Skeptics have said that hope is not a strategy. Agreed. But neither is its absence. We need a sense of hope to animate our plans and actions.

*Contribution:* Robert Frost once said that the brain is a wonderful organ; it starts working the moment you get up in the morning and does not stop until you get into the office. Why does the workplace suck for so many people? In such places people often don't feel like they play an important role in helping the company achieve its aspiration. BetterUp (2019) found that job performance improves 56% when a person feels a strong sense of workplace belonging, and they are 167% more likely to recommend their company to others. Interestingly, performance drops 25% if a person feels excluded.[6] Deloitte (2020) found that belonging strengthens as employees move along a three-step progression from comfort to connection to contribution.[7] Employees gain comfort when they feel like their perspective matters; they feel connected when they relate to colleagues and the company's aspiration; and when they believe their work has meaning, their contribution grows.

Christine Porath (2014) found that employees rate respect as a top leadership behavior, yet more than 50% feel that their workplace does not respect them. Hopefully you're not one of those contributing to this disconnect. Porath's findings should cause you to take notice because employees that feel respected perform better. They report[8]:

- 56% better health

- 1.72 times more trust and safety

- 89% greater job satisfaction

- 92% greater on the job focus

- 1.26 times more meaning and significance

- 1.1 times more likely to stay with their organization

*A word of caution:* don't be lulled into a false belief that everyone should be treated the same. Each person responds to work demands differently so it is incumbent on leaders to be better at knowing the people who work for them, acknowledging their differences, and adapting to them as much as possible. Pace and speed do matter in accomplishing important tasks, but not at the expense of your employees' health. The work will always be there, as will challenges. But when you subject people to the added stress of aggressive time frames you reduce their ability to generate options and original ideas, plus you'll sow the seeds of growing disrespect for your leadership if people perceive you as unprepared or overly reactive.

You can well imagine the benefits from having an aspiration that inspires employees to make great products that also help make a better society. It's hard not to be motivated by that kind of calling. This is especially true for younger generations. Cone Communications found that 94% of Gen Z workers want companies to address important societal issues and, like the PwC workforce survey mentioned in Chapter 4, they consider this to be more important than compensation. Furthermore, your company's aspiration is a visible and important qualifier for even considering whether to work there.[9] When your employees feel invested in your company's aspiration, it shows in their work; they'll be able to better understand and empathize with other stakeholders; and their curiosity will be ignited, which can lead to new ideas that generate societal value.

To encourage and strengthen your employees' contribution, practice the following:

1. Remember that it is not about you. It is about them. Listen to them and help them feel and believe that their work matters but avoid giving empty praise and bromides. Recognize a specific accomplishment, even if it seems relatively innocuous. Small things can have a big impact.

2. The Experience Ambassador behavior from Chapter 3 is important here. Serve as an exemplar of fallibility as it conveys that you are not the All-Being, Master of Time, Space and Dimension (to borrow from Steve Martin) and that you don't expect perfection.[10] But you do encourage progress, which leads to people trying new things even if they don't work out because the real benefit is what is learned, irrespective of success or failure.

3. Recognize that nothing works out as planned, so allow people to handle a project their way. It might not be how you would do it, but it will serve to boost their confidence and sense of agency, which will reap rewards in the future from them as they gain experience.

4. Make it about team and collaboration. This will redirect an employee's energy toward more productive ways to relate to others and reduce the individual pressure on them. That's not to say individual performance isn't important. But we know that, more often than not, the whole is greater than the sum of the parts.

*Agency:* A Web Shandwick study (2017) found that only 19% of employees saw a strong linkage between their actual work versus what their employer described.[11] That should be a warning shot to fix perceptions if for no other reason than employees are your company's ambassadors: their work and their interaction with your stakeholders shape how others see your company. When you give your employees agency, you create the potential for unique perspectives informing better quality decisions and strengthening their commitment to your aspiration. The benefits from giving increased agency take time to mature. Old practices need to be unlearned, replaced with new ones. More mistakes than normal will be made due to something called the "Let Go, Step Up" dynamic.

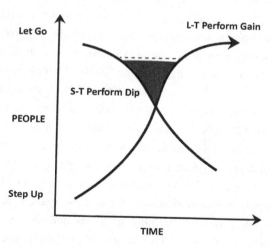

*Source:* Dr Tony O'Driscoll (2015).[12]

"Let Go, Step Up" describes how people must part with comfortable orthodoxies and embrace the practices a new situation requires. For employees *to step up* your leadership team needs to *let go* of some of its decision-making authority. Initially, performance may decline temporarily while people adjust. But the more we practice, the better we get. Performance will start to improve and, over time, increase beyond where it was prior to the change. This can also dramatically reduce the bottlenecks that arose when decisions were concentrated among a few leaders. As Let Go, Step Up shows, employee agency can produce positive organization value, helping people see the connection between their work and your company's aspiration and improving execution of your plans at the local level.

Meta-research of 105 studies conducted by Allan Lee et al. (2017) found that empowering leaders:

- Positively affect employee creativity

- Have higher trust levels than their non-empowering colleagues

- Have more effective impact in Eastern cultures versus Western

Their analysis also showed that less experienced employees saw the biggest performance gains from empowering leadership when compared to more experienced staff.[13]

Bain is among the world's top consultancies and is consistently ranked as a great employer by both Glassdoor and GreatPlacetoWork® for its empowering culture that strongly encourages employees to solve problems at the individual level rather than running approvals up the bureaucratic flagpole. Glassdoor data (2021) on Bain shows more than 4,000 reviews with an average of 4.5 stars out of 5. 92% of Bain employees (called "Bainies") would recommend the company to a friend, and 98% approve of the CEO. A common sentiment is that "a Bainie never lets another Bainie fail," affirming Bain's culture of employee support.[14] Bain is focused on the long-term societal impact of its work and is investing $1 billion in pro bono consulting to improve social impact. They support the Alliance to End Plastic Waste, composed of over 40 companies in the plastics industry that have agreed to invest $1.5 billion to eliminate plastic pollution worldwide over the next five years. In addition, Bain supports social equity, reducing economic inequality and improving education access to underserved communities. Their efforts are producing meaningful value.

Their Social Impact Report 2021 shows that Bain has worked with its clients on 400 + projects to reduce carbon emissions, including conserving 120 million acres and 5,000 miles of vital river ecosystems.[15] Bain is working with Endeavor, an organization devoted to supporting entrepreneurs who want to tackle the world's biggest challenges, and these efforts have created 4.1 million jobs and positively impacted the lives of more than 575 million people.[16] Giving employees agency has helped Bain's social impact strategy.

## MARKET

Employee agency also builds trust with customers. In the first few months of the COVID-19 pandemic companies everywhere were scrambling to salvage their businesses, struggling between sheer survival by cutting costs and jobs at one end of the spectrum, and protecting their employees even at the sacrifice of profits at the other end. By summer 2021, the pandemic had worsened with the spread of the Delta variant. Sadly, those who had not been fully vaccinated saw increasing hospitalizations and rising death rates, straining already fragile healthcare systems, local communities, and company cultures. It's clear what the broader marketplace views as important: 71% of Edelman Trust Barometer (2020) survey respondents said they would lose trust in a brand permanently if it puts profitability ahead of people.[17] That means that underinvesting in the health of employees can ricochet negatively back on your company because customers interpret your stance as tone deaf and insensitive to reality.

COVID-19 isn't your employees' only concern. A US Harris Poll (2021) shows that while 76% of Americans fear new Covid variants, 81% are also concerned about inflation, and 80% worry about mass shootings. The latter are a uniquely US problem that is solvable, but government leaders lack the political courage to take action to protect people.[18] These concerns might seem like unrelated distractions employees shouldn't worry about, but they are all too real and can affect productivity. We simply can't focus on doing good work if we believe our employer lacks concern for our health and safety. Similarly, putting profits ahead of people can also be a sign that a company weighs customer needs as less important, a signal you would want to avoid at all costs unless your objective is to kill your company. This has placed added pressure on CEOs to have their companies be more involved in solving systemic social problems. In fact, Edelman's 2021 Trust Barometer found that 86% of respondents believe CEOs must now lead on societal issues.

> *I expect CEOs to publicly speak out on one or more of these societal challenges: pandemic impact, job automation, societal issues, local community issues.*[19]

As a company leader your role is far more than just delivering financial growth. Create energy around your company's aspiration, show employees why their work matters, and demonstrate that your first concern is for their welfare. The market notices these things. In a Fast Company article Grant Thornton summarized this by saying

> *For companies that are misaligned, the danger can be substantial, resulting in dissatisfied customers...*[20]

Grant Thornton's 2019 Return on Culture survey showed a disturbing disconnect: 75% of executives believe their values are clearly understood, whereas only 33% of employees agree.[21] That lack of alignment has damaging implications your company's reputation. Think of it this way: you might believe you are saying the right things to the market, and perhaps you are, but if those same messages aren't understood by employees, then the chances of you delivering on the promises you make is remote. And the marketplace will eventually detect that discontinuity.

To enhance your organizational value from the market's perspective, address the following:

1. With multiple global crises, employees everywhere are feeling anxious. Understand the issues concerning them. Your compassion will reassure employees and enable them to bring more of their full selves to the workplace.

2. Align your internal and external messaging as this will reduce the chances of you promising one thing but delivering something else.

3. Keep people energized. The market will feed off the energy you and your employees display just as they will feed off any negative vibes you give off.

## ECOSYSTEM

Companies do not operate in a vacuum. They interact with a range of societal institutions: government, the not-for-profit sector, and for-profit partners with specialized capabilities. Having a strong ecosystem brings together organizations with diverse expertise to help address a given need. For the past century, business ecosystems have been used mostly to improve profit maximization, which arguably led to a zero-sum world view in which dominant players dictated unfavorable terms to smaller organizations. That is not a recipe for healthy long-term business relationships or a healthy society.

Boston Consulting Group's Martin Reeves et al. (2019) offer a thoughtful analysis of different business ecosystem types. Within their analysis, they highlight two types: (1) A solution ecosystem; (2) A transaction ecosystem.[22]

Solutions ecosystems are composed of core and complementor firms, each with their own distinct capabilities, that work together to develop a collective solution (the authors cite credit card companies as one example) at a fair price and value.[23] Mark Kramer et al. (2016) argued that businesses in a common ecosystem must join together in a "collective impact" to contribute to the greater public good citing Yara, a Norwegian fertilizer company that operates globally. Yara's mission is to "responsibly feed the world" while protecting the planet. The company is an active supporter of the UN's Sustainable Development Goals. With the world's population projected to increase to nearly 10 billion people by 2050, global food production will need to increase approximately 40%.[24] The challenge is how to do this without also increasing the amount of land or natural resources used. As Yara's leadership states, the collaboration of everyone in the food chain is needed to achieve those dramatic food production increases. In Tanzania in 2009, for example, Yara brought together nearly 70 organizations to develop a $3.4 billion agricultural corridor designed to more reliably help farmers who were otherwise unable to boost crop yields, an enormous problem that exacerbated the country's famine crisis. Yara's fertilizer would offer a major boost in farming efficiency and effectiveness on existing lands. Designed as a 20-year initiative, the project was ahead of schedule by year 3, not only increasing farmer incomes but also helping Yara improve its sales 50%.[25] Yara's efforts to cultivate a productive solutions ecosystem made the difference.

Transactions ecosystems, on the other hand, help link customers with providers (Uber is cited as one example), with transaction fees as the basis for economic value creation. A new company launched by Yara, called the Agoro Carbon Alliance, operates more like an information-based transactions ecosystem, with farmers at the center, enabling them to connect with other farmers and businesses to share the latest practices for reaching important climate and sustainability goals.

Considerations when developing your partner ecosystem:

1. Identify the common societal value opportunity you see that can't be easily addressed separately.

2. Compare your respective organizational values and capabilities to determine how your combined energies can create a multiplier effect.

3. Outline the decision-making model ecosystem partners must agree to and how you will resolve differences.

4. Determine performance incentives for all ecosystem members.

5. Develop a code of conduct expected of each ecosystem member.

6. Conduct a regular ecosystem health audit and review meetings to pursue improvements.

## So What?

Anthony Guerrero learned the importance of building a collaborative business system with his paper route and the value of shared community interest from baseball and burritos. Those are powerful lessons. Yet we tend to lose sight of them as we grow older. The beauty of Anthony's experiences is that they remind us of where value lies. Not just with us, but with colleagues and community members. When you're transforming your business into a force for good, think of Anthony. You might be running a multi-billion-dollar global enterprise but that doesn't diminish the importance of collaboration and community in generating meaningful and measurable organization value – that's as true for a paper route as it is for a multinational company. Now we'll explore why pursuing societal value is crucial to your business in Chapter 7.

## NOTES

1. Malik, R. (2015). The message of Mahatma Gandhi. Economy, culture & history. *Japan Spotlight BiMonthly*, *34*(3), 48–51. Retrieved from https://web.p.ebscohost.com/abstract?direct=true&profile=ehost&scope=site&authtype=crawler&jrnl=13489216&AN=114543889&h=0cKljLD3X1zzufQpQhUjf25Cum7KOl%2fx35fwSZfP1LBiSU4RhaS0s9YcP%2fcBv5BdWOUvDMQ8cksfU6wUsvzA7Q%3d%3d&crl=c&resultNs=AdminWebAuth&resultLocal=ErrCrlNotAuth&crlhashurl=login.aspx%3fdirect%3dtrue%26profile%3dehost%26scope%3dsite%26authtype%3dcrawler%26jrnl%3d13489216%26AN%3d114543889.
2. Based on 2021 author Interviews with Anthony Guerrero.
3. Multiple sources: (1) Kotter, J. (2011). Does corporate culture drive financial performance? *Forbes*. Retrieved from https://www.forbes.com/sites/johnkotter/2011/02/10/does-corporate-culture-drive-financial-performance/?sh=12942ff67e9e; (2) Kotter, J., & James, H. (2008). Corporate culture and performance. Chapter 2, Exhibits 2.3, 2.4. 2.5. Retrieved from https://www.amazon.com/Corporate-Culture-Performance-John-Kotter-ebook/dp/B0033C58EU/ref=sr_1_1?dchild=1&keywords=john+kotter+james+heskett&qid=1628539443&s=books&sr=1-1&asin=B0033C58EU&revisionId=&format=2&depth=1.
4. Berman, M., Jenny, D.-P., John, H., Adélaïde, H., & Tracy, T. (2020). Giving people hope by reigniting your company purpose. Bain. Retrieved from https://www.bain.com/insights/giving-people-hope-by-igniting-your-company-purpose/.
5. Mattis, J. S. (2021). Five strategies for cultivating hope this year. *The Conversation*. Retrieved from https://theconversation.com/5-strategies-for-cultivating-hope-this-year-152523.
6. No author. (2019). BetterUp's new, industry-leading research shows companies that fail at belonging lose tens of millions in revenue. BetterUp. Retrieved from https://www.betterup.com/press/betterups-new-industry-leading-research-shows-companies-that-fail-at-belonging-lose-tens-of-millions-in-revenue.
7. Volini, E., Schwart, J., Mallon, D., Van Durme, Y., Hauptmann, M., Yan, R., & Poynton, S. (2020). Belonging: From comfort to connection to contribution. Deloitte. Retrieved from https://www2.deloitte.com/us/en/insights/focus/human-capital-trends/2020/creating-a-culture-of-belonging.html.
8. Porath, C. (2014). Half of employees don't feel respected by their bosses. *Harvard Business Review*, p. 1. Retrieved from https://www.hbsp.harvard.edu/download?url=%2Fcatalog%2Fsample%2FH012O0-PDF-ENG%2Fcontent&metadata=eyJlcnJvck1lc3NhZ2UiOiJZb3UgbXVzdCBiZSByZWdpc3Rlc

mVkIGFzIGEgUHJlbWl1bSBFZHVjYXRvciBvbiB0aGlzIHdlYiBzaXRlIHRv
IHNlZSBFZHVjYXRvciBDb3BpZXMgYW5kIEZyZWUgVHJpYWxzLiBOb
3QgcmVnaXN0ZXJlZD8gQXBwbHkgb3RoLiBBBY2Nlc3MgZXhwaXJlZD8
gUmVhdXRob3JpemUgbm93LiJ9.

9.  RippleMatch. (2020). 35 companies with powerful social impact initiatives.
    RippleMatch. Retrieved from https://ripplematch.com/journal/article/com
    panies-with-powerful-social-impact-initiatives-65f368a5/.

10. Martin, S. (1978). Let's get small monologue. Saturday Night Live. Retrieved
    from https://www.nbc.com/saturday-night-live/video/steve-martin-monolog
    ue-lets-get-small/3004269.

11. No author. (2017). Weber Shandwick and KRC research. Brand credibility
    gap: Bridging the divide. Retrieved from https://www.webershandwick.com/
    uploads/news/files/EmployerBrandCredibilityGap.pdf.

12. O'Driscoll, T. (2015). Overcome paradigm paralysis with courage, confidence
    and conviction. Training. Retrieved from https://trainingmag.com/overcome-
    paradigm-paralysis-with-courage-confidence-and-conviction/.

13. Lee, A., Sara, W., & Amy, W. T. (2018). When empowering employees
    works, and when it doesn't. Harvard Business Review. Retrieved from
    https://www.hbsp.harvard.edu/download?url=%2Fcatalog%2Fsample%
    2FH046XV-PDF-ENG%2Fcontent&metadata=eyJlcnJvck1lc3NhZ2UiOi
    JZb3UgbXVzdCBiZSByZWdpc3RlcmVkIGFzIGEgUHJlbWl1bSBFZHVj
    YXRvciBvbiB0aGlzIHdlYiBzaXRlIHRvIHNlZSBFZHVjYXRvciBDb3Bp
    ZXMgYW5kIEZyZWUgVHJpYWxzLiBOb3QgcmVnaXN0ZXJlZD8gQ
    XBwbHkgb3RoLiBBBY2Nlc3MgZXhwaXJlZD8gUmVhdXRob3JpemUg
    bm93LiJ9.

14. Glassdoor. Bain & Company. (2021). Retrieved from https://www.glassdoor.
    com/Reviews/Bain-and-Company-Reviews-E3752.htm.

15. No author. (2021). Bain impact report, p. 10. Retrieved from https://www.
    bain.com/globalassets/noindex/2021/bain_report_impact_report_2021.pdf.

16. See footnote 15, p. 24.

17. Edelman, R. (2020). Trust barometer special report: Brand trust and the
    coronavirus pandemic. Edelman. Retrieved from https://www.edelman.com/
    research/covid-19-brand-trust-report.

18. Gerzema, J., & Will, J. (2021). The Harris Poll. Retrieved from http://
    theharrispoll-8654532.hs-sites.com/the-insight-wave-75.

19. Edelman, R. (2021). Edelman trust barometer 2021. Edelman. Retrieved
    from https://www.edelman.com/trust/2021-trust-barometer.

20. Grant Thornton. (2019). Are your company's brand and culture aligned?
    Fast Company. Retrieved from https://www.fastcompany.com/90355383/are-
    your-companys-brand-and-culture-aligned.

21. Multiple sources: (1) See footnote 20. (2) Grant Thornton. (2019). Culture &
    cash connection: New report ties revenue growth to companies with healthy
    cultures. Grant Thornton. Retrieved from https://www.grantthornton.com/
    library/press-releases/2019/april/culture-cash-connection.aspx.

22. Pidun, U., Martin, R., & Maximilian, S. (2019). Do you need a business
    ecosystem? Boston Consulting Group. Retrieved from https://www.bcg.
    com/en-us/publications/2019/do-you-need-business-ecosystem.

23. See footnote 22.

24. No author. Yara (2021). Driving sustainable agriculture in Europe-it starts with the farmer. Retrieved from https://www.yara.com/crop-nutrition/sustainable-agriculture-in-europe/.

25. Kramer, M. R., & Pfitzer, M. W. (2016). The ecosystem of shared value. *Harvard Business Review*. Retrieved from https://www.hbsp.harvard.edu/download?url=%2Fcatalog%2Fsample%2FR1610G-PDF-ENG%2Fcontent&metadata=eyJlcnJvck1lc3NhZ2UiOiJZb3UgbXVzdCBiZSByZWdpc3RlcmVkIGFzIGEgUHJlbWl1bSBFZHVjYXRvciBvbiB0aGlzIHdlYiBzaXRlIHRvIHNlZSBFZHVjYXRvciBDb3B5cXMgYW5kIEZyZWUgVHJpYWxzLiBOb3QgcgVnaXN0ZXJlZD8gQXBwbHkgbm93LiBBY2Nlc3MgZXhwaXJlZD8gUmVhdXRob3JpemUgbm93LiJ9.

# 7

# GENERATING SOCIETAL VALUE

*We become just by doing just acts, temperate by doing temperate acts, brave by doing brave acts.*[1]

*–Aristotle*

Mac McKenzie has societal value figured out. Through his work as Managing Director of Bridge Partnership (Asia Pacific), a global firm specializing in organizational transformation and leadership development, and Founder of the Bridge Institute (Bridge Partnership's not-for-profit arm), he is devoted to his work, his clients, his colleagues, his stakeholders, and his family. He is one of those people whom the moment you meet you can't help but like and immediately admire. It's not just because he is friendly and fascinating, but because when you talk to him you sense that underlying his approachable demeanor is a person deeply and utterly committed to serving others. It permeates every fiber of his being. Mac exudes a calm, reflective energy that belies the incredibly difficult problems he and his colleagues help to solve. When he speaks he does so with the humility of someone who has worked in some of the more difficult hotspots (including central Asia, South Asia and South-East Asia) on behalf of hugely critical human crises and fully understands that he does not have all the answers. Bridge Partnership was founded 30 years ago and delivers world-class solutions for leaders and their organizations, helping them become a stronger force for good in the world. Under Mac's leadership, the Bridge Institute works at the community and societal level to help people solve intractable problems *together* (for instance, stopping violence in societies, creating passive immunity solutions for Covid-19, helping victims of sexual assault, advancing the UN's 17 Sustainable Development Goals…), working with people to solve issues collectively, then giving them the tools and collaborative confidence to continue doing this themselves. As a case in point, the Bridge Institute spent time in a country working with local groups to help them overcome social tensions and ongoing strife. In one of the groups was a young man whose father was killed during an uprising. He had devoted himself to avenging his death and saw the violence that took his father as a reason to pursue more violence in his name. The Bridge Institute worked with him and his associates on the social beliefs and political factors that had reinforced a culture of violence, getting them to discuss the tensions openly. As familiarity grew, they gained new insights from Mac and his colleagues about the benefits of a nonviolent, peacebuilding mindset. The result helped the groups ease tensions. And he came away dedicated to nonviolence and is now an active advocate for peace where he lives. Mac and his colleagues focus on civil rights by bringing together the youth in vulnerable regions to focus on developing their leadership capabilities through joint projects aimed at peacebuilding, helping them become advocates for social justice and agents for peaceful change.

There's a reason Mac is so good at connecting with other people and creating meaningful societal value: he believes in it to his very core, and he is also a gifted facilitator. He invites, he provokes, he encourages, he listens, and he enjoys the perspectives everyone brings into whatever setting he is in. I've been fortunate to have taught with Mac in leadership programs in Asia and have seen him create an atmosphere of trust that inspires people to be open. His quiet, reassuring outward confidence belies an internal restlessness to help people who are dealing with a mind-numbing range of challenges, from organizational culture change initiatives to horribly disturbing human rights violations within communities. Mac is tireless, traveling around the world to change mindsets and energize people to overcome entrenched beliefs and apply new practices while fostering healthier community dialogues. He and his wife aim to instil a strong sense of societal commitment in their children, introducing them to different cultures and their challenges. And, as if his family and work needs weren't already full-time activities, Mac is also a keen mountain climber, having climbed peaks in the Andes, the Himalayas, the Sierra Nevadas, the Southern Alps and the European Alps. What you learn from Mac is that his family, his work, and his mountain climbing are not solo efforts. Achievement requires a team of collaborators to help with an incredibly diverse array of situations. To address the intractable problems he deals with, Mac brings together government, business and civic leaders into a partner ecosystem that helps people expand their thinking. Mac doesn't have the answers, nor does he pretend that he does. But he does know the importance and power of bringing disparate, divergent groups together to address vexing, complex problems. His professional and personal lives share a common aspiration: to do something good that is meaningful to others. As Mac says, "if you don't stand for something good then you risk your entire existence." Lest you be skeptical of Mac's intentions, be assured he is not a virtue signaler; he's a virtue practitioner. Mac is a good news story... powerful and inspiring, and a reassuring reminder that there are remarkable people in the world devoted to ensuring that leaders and organizations do well by doing good for society.[2]

## SOCIETAL VALUE FACTORS

Can you measure societal value? Not yet, at least not precisely. This is a question frequently asked about the "S" (social) in ESG. Precise measures do vary, which frustrates investors. Pinpointing its impact is also tricky, and prone to misunderstanding and imprecision. It helps to first think about what we mean by societal value and the "S" in ESG. They are a set of actions designed to enhance the quality of life and well-being of the communities you serve. That still doesn't lend itself to a simple metric. As those I've interviewed have commented, measuring a person's quality of life or well-being is like assigning a numerical satisfaction value to love – you can't, at least not precisely. Yet they admit they can tell when their societal value quotient is lagging because their company isn't part of the community's social milieu. But measuring the absence of something is problematic. When your company is absent from the local community's life, it's as if you were never there in the first place. That is hardly reassuring to investors, or customers, or employees. But what is reassuring is that change is coming. Some of the world's largest investment funds and regulatory bodies are beginning to ask companies to track and disclose their ESG scorecards which will help us get closer to measuring it. Improving societal value is a key reason why.

We know that consumers want companies to do far more than they currently do to contribute to societal value. The Black Lives Matter (BLM) movement that began in the US (and has since grown worldwide) is one example. Citizens not only protested, but they implored businesses to take an active role in eliminating social injustice in hiring and performance management practices. The messages communicated and products sold must reflect our better angels and loudly signal that injustice of any kind will not be tolerated by any company anywhere. If appealing to your sense of humanity isn't enough, then consider this: fixing racial injustice once and for all has enormous economic consequences. Estimates show a potential $8 trillion increase in GDP by 2050 by closing the racial equity gap.[3]

We know the evidence is strong that consumers of all ages believe it is important for companies to have a bigger commitment to social responsibility, especially Millennials, who are going to be the dominate economic and social power for the next few decades. Societal value is also good for investors. 73% say that efforts to be socially responsible and a force for good contribute positively to return on their investments.[4] At the same time, only 36% of consumers trust business leaders to do what is right.[5] That means businesses have significant potential upside from addressing this low level of trust by demonstrably improving their societal value contributions.

Societal value and social responsibility shouldn't be contrary to a business's success, yet they are too often relegated to a lower priority list, to be considered when times are good and financial performance is strong. This narrow perspective suggests that being socially responsible is situational, and such an approach is the result of company leaders who don't fully understand the importance of societal value to their company's long-term financial success.

## Internal Measures for Societal Value

Larry Fink is Chairman and CEO of Blackrock, the world's largest investment company with over $9 trillion in assets under management. He and Blackrock have outsized influence on the global marketplace, so it was especially noteworthy when, in 2018, Fink said

> *Society is demanding that companies, both public and private, serve a social purpose. To prosper over time, every company must not only deliver financial performance, but also show it makes a positive contribution to society.*[6]

In 2020 Fink emphasized that climate change will be a "defining factor" determining whether a company succeeds or fails. His 2021 Shareholder Letter said that companies must describe how they will contribute to a net-zero economy, with explicit guidance that companies show how they have integrated this into their long-term strategy. Each of the ESG elements feeds into each other and, as Fink says,

> Questions of racial justice, economic inequality or community engagement are often classed as an S issue in E.S.G. conversations...But it is misguided to draw such stark lines between these categories. For example, climate change is already having a disproportionate impact on low-income communities around the world – is that an E or an S issue?

BlackRock has also stated it now requires companies to disclose a wide range of social issues, including race, gender, ethnicity. Furthermore, CEO Larry Fink's 2021 letter to CEOs wants company sustainability reports linked to their plans for diversity, equity, and inclusion, essentially their "S" in ESG scores.[7] The numbers and percentages are important, and easy to measure, in your total employee population, and BlackRock's requirement will undoubtedly be further enhanced, compelling businesses to track these areas, and adjacent factors, more responsibly. There is no question that your company's reputation will be affected by the decisions you make on behalf of the societal value motive. To Mac McKenzie's point, you must stand for something good; otherwise why are you here? Doing what BlackRock requires is crucial, but only addresses part of the societal value need. Further strengthening occurs when the quality of engagement from your employees with the local communities is perceived as positive, noticeable and notable.

So, how engaged are you with the communities and markets you serve? This is not a question that asks whether you are donating money to your favorite causes, although financial contribution is certainly noteworthy. Instead, societal value is realized when your company is more than just an employer selling products and services; it must be considered an invaluable contributor to the lifeblood of that community, where your employees serve alongside other societal actors in supporting and even providing services that fuel the community's sense of social connectedness. Societal value is the heart, soul, and intellectual rationale for the role businesses can and must play in the world, and it underscores the need for businesses to become a force for good, not just a maker of goods. After all, if your company is not contributing positively to society, then why does it exist at all? But what can get in the way are the innumerable day-to-day tasks of running the business, of not upsetting those routines that currently help your company earn its keep, and of not disrupting how people get their work done. It becomes too hard to create the kind of change needed, even though evidence shows that greater societal contribution leads to better outcomes for your company and the world. If you are struggling with the decision of investing in and reimagining how your company can become a force for good, you are not alone. But even though it is hard, don't let convenient excuses prevent your company from becoming profoundly more positive, consequential and impactful to society.

## External Measures for Societal Value

Making great products and services and providing jobs are important, but only part of being a good corporate citizen, because these contributions will be short-lived if your relationships with the larger community are toxic. You must broaden your definition of contribution to society by including:

1. *How you manage ecosystem partner relationships*
   The health of your company will be greatly affected by the health of your partner ecosystem. Think of it this way: if you hang out with people who are committed to health and fitness it will be hard for you to not be influenced by them and becoming more health conscious yourself. A healthy ecosystem reinforces the healthy ambitions you have for your company.
   There are three ecosystem dimensions to regularly evaluate and audit:
   - Health of partner relationships: how trusted are the partners and what criteria will you and your partners use to guide good behavior in the ecosystem?

   - Financial health: how financially stable are partners and what mechanisms are required for evaluating when struggling partners should receive support from other partners, or wind-down their participation until they regain stability? What aggregate value do ecosystem partners expect to gain from each other and how will the results be shared?

- Community vibrancy: what will indicate that the ecosystem has contributed real value to the well-being and quality of life in targeted communities?

2. *Human rights policies and practices*
Treating your employees well and with respect is a no brainer. So too is extending that philosophy to how your company does business. Selling your offerings to people or countries or companies that violate human rights is effectively condoning those abusive practices. Your company's growth is not about doing "whatever it takes" but is instead about doing "the right thing". There are macro and micro factors for you to evaluate:

- Macro: Is your business ecosystem selling to buyers known or suspected of human rights violations? The UN provides a useful definition of human rights, encompassing economic, social, cultural, civil, and political criteria.[8] Adapting these to your business's values and corresponding ecosystem partners' practices is a sensible expectation and will help clarify acceptable and unacceptable performance.

- Micro: What is your business doing to ensure diversity, equity, and inclusion that goes beyond employee population data to include acceptable and unacceptable values-based behaviors?

3. *Your company's reputation for business ethics*
If you allow amoral and unethical behavior with employees, partners, and customers then you are saying profit is more important than people or principles. That doesn't bode well for your company going forward. Will there be buyers and markets for irresponsible practices? Unfortunately, yes. But it will be reduced to a fraction of the total business activity and, as practitioners of economic and social good multiply, so too will the ability to transform responsible economic activity into positive social contribution, relegating those lacking ethics to minor, marginal, and shunned areas of society. Ethics are a BIG values-based area. Examine it through these meta-themes:

- Your company's values

- How those values are exemplified by employee behaviors

- How those values are mirrored by ecosystem partners and target market opportunities

- How your company addresses values-lapses and shares the lessons learned both internally and externally

4. *The sense of genuine societal involvement your company is perceived to bring to the communities it serves.*
This one is easy. When people in the local community talk about your company, is it to share praise or derision? The former suggests that your company is viewed as an important supporter of the community whereas the latter signals your company is abusing the generosity and goodwill of the community whose resources you share.

   - What explicit actions does your company perform that improve the quality of life among the communities it serves?

   - What specific criteria will you use to determine the impact to community well-being (disease eradication, environmental health, education attainment, economic equality, social justice...)?

## Building Communities

There are two primary types of communities your company can help cultivate to build societal value: brand communities; and local communities.

### Brand Communities

When your company inspires extraordinary devotion in its users and followers, then it is likely because they find a shared sense of values, expressed through your brand. This dedication is more than just the use of your offerings; followers often associate the positive attributes of your company to their personal identity. Note that building a brand community for your company is not a marketing exercise; it is a whole-business strategy that encompasses how your company engages with the market and creates a dialogue with stakeholders, plus whether people are attracted to your company because of the values and practices it demonstrates. Brand communities are not characterized by rigid conformity in thoughts and actions among its members. The sign of a healthy brand community is when inspiring debate and camaraderie occurs regularly, motivating members to rally others in support of a particular societal need, or to simply help the brand make corrections. Community members are a powerful force, yet they are not controlled by the company. Success is an outgrowth of the resonance followers have with the brand and its relative standing in the world as a symbolic platform for expressing ideas.

**Brand Community Guidelines**

1. Don't force a community structure onto your stakeholders. Listen carefully to find out which factors attract them to your company. Remember, not all community members are customers, or shareholders. They may just be believers in the way you conduct your business and societal outreach.

2. Don't approach brand communities as a short-term marketing communications ploy to spike sales. Members of brand communities are in it for the long haul, so encourage thoughtful participation from all stakeholders.

3. Don't drive the community conversation. Merely participate, be attentive.

4. Don't try to advertise your way into a brand community structure.

**Local Communities**

Wherever your company does business, you are a *potentially* important societal contributor to that community. *Potentially* is italicized because merely selling your wares and employing a few people in the local market does not make you an accepted community member or trusted corporate citizen. To be considered part of the fabric of the community, you must be involved, beyond employment and economic contribution. When smart global companies open new offices, there is usually a multiyear plan that includes how to make their presence in that market successful by learning how business is conducted there. Consider your own approach to traveling to new areas. Travel stimulates eye-opening awareness of everything that is new. If you are fortunate enough to live in another country, then you'll find that your ability to experience that culture and understand differences deepens further. You might not always agree with other people's perspectives, but the very act of listening to them and being open to other perspectives helps strengthen your understanding of that community. In my own case, living in Asia for 15 years broadened my perspective and strengthened my appreciation for the rich traditions that give each country a sense of identity. Early on I found myself acutely aware of and fascinated by the innumerable differences of each culture. I learned to see and experience each country through local eyes and practices.

The antithesis of a good community are groups that close debate and shut down social dialogues simply because they disagree with points of view different from their own. The current populist movements in many western democracies, sadly, exemplify communities that detract from societal value because they advocate for retrograde social views and exclusionary beliefs that do nothing to advance modern civilization and, instead, provoke incivility and promote divisiveness. That doesn't seem to be a recipe for personal, let alone business, success.

What does societal value look like when practiced? Some examples:

### Elsevier

Founded 140 years ago, Elsevier is a Netherlands-based research and healthcare information analytics company that publishes 2,650 journals worldwide, accounting for 18% of research and 27% of citations in the field. Elsevier has a gift matching program for societal causes that employees support. The company supports employee initiatives on a wide range of social issues including DE&I, disabilities, gender equality, and LGTBQ. With its expertise in research and healthcare, the company has developed corresponding partnerships with organizations to help communities that are historically underserved. Employees also get two volunteer days per year to support a cause of their choice.[9] Elsevier's efforts underscore the importance the company places on its employees being a force for good wherever they are.

### Jones Lang Lasalle (JLL)

JLL is a global real estate firm headquartered in Chicago, and it contributes to six of the UN's Sustainable Development Goals (Good Health and Well-Being; Gender Equality; Decent Work and Economic Growth; Sustainable Cities and Communities; Responsible Consumption and Production; Climate Action), integrating these with the company's business planning, then publicly reporting the results each year. People development is geared toward societal stewardship, encouraging employees to participate and support community activities wherever they are in the world, plus they have the autonomy to choose which issues mean the most to them. This more personal approach to community engagement helps local communities view JLL in a more positive light since they are seeing the genuine commitment of the firm's employees in local markets.

## MAS Holdings

MAS Holdings is a Sri Lankan apparel manufacturer founded in 1986 by three brothers: Mahesh, Ajay, and Sharad Amelian. They have since become one of the world's highest-quality apparel companies, supplying apparel for leading brands like Puma, Ralph Lauren, Patagonia, and Columbia, and PPE medical apparel for global healthcare workers including those fighting Covid-19. The company started an innovative HR program in 2003 called "Women Go Beyond," which recognizes the achievements of its female-majority workforce in their contributions at work and in the communities they serve. The company has fostered a deep connection with Sri Lankans as well as their other operations around the world due to the unyielding commitment to empowering women, wherever they are, to be great colleagues and community contributors.

## SO WHAT?

Focusing on societal value improves the potential for greater economic gain that enhances the well-being of people in society and can improve your company's reputation and performance, beyond narrow measures of business profitability and shareholder wealth. A 2020 Kantar Purpose Survey studied companies over a 12-year period. Those companies perceived as having a high positive impact to society generated brand value growth of 175% versus companies with medium positive impact (86%) and those with low positive impact (70%).[10] Friede et al.'s 2015 study provided further evidence about the value creation benefits resulting from companies that emphasize ESG investments[11]:

- 44% of companies cited growth opportunities as the reason for investing in ESG initiatives.

- 33% of profits are at risk from government "intervention" if companies do not invest in ESG.

- ESG-focused companies, where employees perceived their work as meaningful and connected to the greater good the company offers, saw higher stock returns of 2.3–3.8% per year.

You wouldn't be human if you didn't have doubts about pursuing a new business model fit for the needs of the twenty-first century. A 2020 study of 150 CEOs by Heidrick & Struggles in partnership with the Saïd Business School at Oxford University affirmed that societal changes and challenges are impacting the CEO's role like never before, exacerbating the anxiety and tension they feel. When asked if they ever doubt themselves, 71% said yes. But doubt can inspire curiosity and spark insight, too.[12]

> Doubts are to CEOs what nerves are to elite athletes: a source of focus and insight when harnessed constructively, a threat to peak performance when not...doubt is a capability to be cultivated rather than a weakness to be cured.[13]

Interestingly, doubt can be both a toxin and antidote. Think about how you react when you feel doubt, stress, or anxiety. Doubt's toxic effects can force you into a fetal position in the corner if you let them. But doubt can sharpen your focus on how to best accomplish change. Because we can actually *feel* the impact of doubt on our physical and emotional well-being, we lean into reducing its discomfort more than supporting the intellectual and psychological benefits we know would result from increasing our efforts to help society.[14] It *feels* better faster to relieve the emotional toll rather than pursue the harder work and longer pathway to solving a vexing problem. And that's where the rub is when dealing with how to transform our businesses. It is SO much more emotionally satisfying to see the money flow in from something we've built, reaping the rewards from our hard work to this point. We understandably should feel good – that's akin to a sugar high. Yet for our business's longer-term benefits we also must put in the effort to build a stronger, healthier, and more agile organization that positively impacts the world by improving the well-being and quality of life for the communities we serve. Financial value is enhanced by demonstrating superb reputational, organizational, and societal value, along with leveraging consumer, regulatory and financial market trends, as we'll see in Chapter 8.

# NOTES

1. Aristotle. (350 BCE). The Nicomachean ethics, Book II: Moral virtue. Translated by W.D. Ross (p. 1). Retrieved from http://www.pgliterarytranslation.com/resources/NicomacheanEthics_BookII.pdf.
2. Based on 2021 author Interviews with Mac McKenzie.
3. Turner, A. (2018). The business case for racial equity. W. K. Kellogg Foundation. pp. 3, 8–9. Retrieved from http://www.nationalcivicleague.org/wp-content/uploads/2018/04/RacialEquityNationalReport-kellogg.pdf.
4. Stobierski, T. (2021). 15 Eye-opening corporate social responsibility statistics. Harvard Business School online. Retrieved from https://online.hbs.edu/blog/post/corporate-social-responsibility-statistics.
5. No author. (2018). 2018 world value index. Enso (p. 18). Retrieved from https://www.enso.co/wp-content/uploads/2018/09/World-Value-Index-2018-Brand-Report-enso.pdf.
6. Sorkin, A. R. (2018) BlackRock's message: Contribute to society, or risk losing our support. *New York Times.* Retrieved from: https://www.nytimes.com/2018/01/15/business/dealbook/blackrock-laurence-fink-letter.html.
7. Sisul, E. (2021). The "S" in ESG. *Forbes.* Retrieved from https://www.forbes.com/sites/guidehouse/2021/04/06/the-s-in-esg/.
8. (No date). United Nations-Peace, dignity and equality on a healthy planet. Retrieved from https://www.un.org/en/global-issues/human-rights.
9. Multiple sources: 1. No author. (2020). 12 Companies with Amazing community support programs. Comparably. Retrieved from https://www.comparably.com/news/12-companies-with-amazing-community-support-programs/; 2. No author. (2021). Fast Facts Download about Elsevier. Retrieved from https://www.elsevier.com/__data/assets/pdf_file/0005/1095953/Fast-Facts.pdf.
10. Purpose 2020. Igniting purpose-led growth. Kantar Consulting. Retrieved from https://consulting.kantar.com/wp-content/uploads/2019/06/Purpose-2020-PDF-Presentation.pdf.
11. Friede, G., & Busch, T. (2015). ESG and financial performance: Aggregated evidence from more than 2000 empirical studies. Journal of Sustainable Finance & Investment. Column 5, Issue 4. Retrieved from https://www.tandfonline.com/doi/full/10.1080/20430795.2015.1118917.
12. Smets, M., Morris, T., & White, A., Athanasopoulou, A., Cowan, A. M., Germain, V., Tullett, D., & West, K. (2015). The CEO report-embracing the paradoxes of leadership and the power of doubt. Heidrick and Struggles. Said Business School University of Oxford. (pp. 14–16). Retrieved from https://www.sbs.ox.ac.uk/sites/default/files/2018-09/The-CEO-Report-Final.pdf.
13. See footnote 12.
14. Kross, E. Chatter. (2021). The voice in our head, why it matters, and how to harness it (p. 21) ©2021 Crown Books.

# 8

# DELIVERING FINANCIAL VALUE

*There are no shortcuts to the top of the palm tree.*[1]
*—Cameroonian Proverb*

"People everywhere are talking about ESG because there is a big swirl around the promise of changing the world," says Kate Gordon. She knows this well because Kate has extensive policy background from both the private and public sectors. Her interest in climate issues developed as an outgrowth of her early career work in economic equity, influenced by her role as Editor of the Labor and Employment Law Journal while in law school at UC Berkeley. Early in her career she was involved in clean energy to support US domestic energy security and to create jobs. She became interested in climate change through focusing on identifying, analyzing, and communicating the economic risks associated with the climate crisis. She was Founding Executive Director and Lead Author of the Risky Business Project, a bipartisan initiative to engage business leaders on the economic risks associated with climate change, reframing it as an economic issue, not a political one. She worked with co-Chairs Hank Paulson (former US Secretary of the Treasury), Michael Bloomberg (Founder of Bloomberg, former New York City Mayor, former US Presidential candidate), Tom Steyer (Founder of Farallon Capital, former US Presidential candidate) and other key influencers on this effort. Kate's expertise has also included working in US national and state-level positions as Senior Advisor to the US Energy Secretary, and Director of the Governor's Office of Planning and Research for the State of California. She points out that concern for the climate crisis is not a PR stunt for companies or a way for them to get on the global stage to make bold proclamations, nor is limited to the scientific community, nor should it be relegated to the sustainability department in some distant corner of the business. It is an existential threat to the planet and to all economic actors within, from governments to businesses to NGOs. Kate has seen the global conversation about the climate crisis evolve from being fringe, to being driven by the scientific and environmental communities, to becoming important for societal institutions to start tackling (government, business, NGOs, community groups…) to support improved quality of life and well-being needs for people everywhere. The climate crisis, and the other converging crises (Covid-19, social injustice, economic inequality…) are no longer distant abstractions affecting other people elsewhere. They are pocketbook issues: whether those are felt through the impact to your company's bottom line from disrupted supply chains, increased raw materials costs, relocated facilities, remote work, and consequently discussed in the boardroom; or they are felt by each of us individually in our lighter wallets resulting from increased pass-through costs. The aggregate impact of more virulent diseases, rising social tensions, increasing severity and unpredictability of storms, worsening wildfires worldwide, melting polar ice caps, and the rapid acidification of ocean environments from increased carbon in the atmosphere directly affects normal economic and business channels, making supply, delivery, and support less reliable and ultimately raising the costs that all of us pay.

Despite the enormous challenge, Kate is clear-eyed that the climate crisis is a big tent opportunity. With her extensive experience working on climate and economic issues in government, think tanks and business, Kate has seen what works and what doesn't. She has been instrumental in bringing key societal actors together to tackle wicked problems, and the enormous complexities involved in transitioning to a cleaner, more sustainable path for the world remains a work in progress. One of the challenges about the global climate conversation is that it has been dominated by the environmental community for such a long time that a strong anti-industry bias has driven the conversation, often colored by the belief that transforming from fossil fuels to renewables like solar energy and wind turbines are an easy fix. Kate knows from her work the past 20 years that climate change and pollution are enormous problems with no easy fix, and that demonizing industry writ large is a nonstarter. We cannot change decisions already made from countless companies the past 100 years, but we can change what companies do going forward. And that means business must have a seat at the solution table, not excluded from it. But businesses need incentives to participate. There is no question about the importance of renewables as the future of energy. The problem is that manufacturing organizations must still make those wind turbines and solar farms, and their components are dominated by industrial-based materials (steel, for example, as well as the silicon used in solar cells). Given this, the real opportunity lies in helping industry rapidly evolve toward cleaner practices, innovative manufacturing techniques and far better industrial efficiency since we can't easily flip a switch to shut down heavy manufacturing and simultaneously turn on more sustainable, earth-friendly replacements (see the description of Divergent 3D Founder Kevin Czinger work in Chapter 12. His manufacturing innovations represent the kind of new thinking that can accelerate the transformation from twentieth century models to twenty-first century ones).

That's a question of money and it will inevitably affect financial value for all of us worldwide. Capital must be available to invest in sustainability, there must be a return on those investments, and the outcomes must also strengthen the company's reputation and attract new customers. We know that Black-Rock sees climate change as a defining factor for their investment decisions by putting ESG at the forefront of its investment criteria, with the goal of portfolio companies achieving net zero carbon emissions by 2050.[2] TPG is another example: with over $108 billion in assets under management, the firm launched its Impact Platform in 2016, focused on societally-based investments, including its TPG Rise Climate fund that raised $5.4 billion in 2021 to invest in climate solutions.[3] There are other promising signals as well. A comprehensive paper by Marc Gerber et al. (2021) said that by mid-2021 in Europe the market for green bonds had doubled from 2020, to between $400 billion and $500 billion. Non-investment grade sustainability notes, a new investment vehicle in 2021, captured investor enthusiasm, attracting nearly €3.5 billion as of June 2021. Concerns over greenwashing led to the International Capital Market Association issuing new green and social bond principles to improve ESG transparency.[4] The European Commission set into law targets to reduce greenhouse gases by 55% of 1990 levels by 2030,[5] and the US Securities and Exchange Commission (SEC) is working on new climate disclosure requirements as of this writing.[6] These various regulatory efforts are bringing sharper definition to ESG reporting expectations for companies which will increase the attention paid to what businesses are doing versus claiming, which will help improve our insight into actual societal contribution from companies.

Scientists and environmentalists are expert at identifying the problems, collecting data, setting evidence-based targets, and explaining what life will be like if we don't change. But designing the transition from where we have been to where we need to go is not their expertise. That's why businesses play a critical role because they are seeing and experiencing the effects of the climate crisis every day on their bottom lines, which will only worsen if we pretend that business as usual is the answer. Businesses can translate the scientific findings into implementation planning and actions. And the partnership between scientists, environmentalists, government, NGOs and community groups and businesses will have a direct impact on financial value.

## TODAY'S FINANCIAL VALUE

We once considered growing financial value as the purpose of a business. But the reality is that financial value indicates how well your company delivers on its reputational, organizational, and societal value dimensions. Kate Gordon's point that industry needs to be included, not excluded, in initiatives to improve global sustainability is important, partly because businesses are embedded deeply across the world, in every society and economic system, so new sustainability-based business models can quickly shift social patterns toward green adoption; and partly because businesses are effective at attracting vast amounts of capital to fund growth. That capital must now be deployed to fund ESG innovation. As investors gain confidence and see a business model that can be scaled, attracting more capital becomes easier.

Sources of capital are changing. Your company must pay attention to the criteria investors are using. Retail investors have more momentum now compared to institutional investors, doubling in volume during the pandemic to 20% of total equity trades. Fueled by zero-based commission trading introduced by several of the largest investment brokerages in 2019, individual traders jumped into the market.[7] Schwab research (2021) found that the median age of retail investors since 2020 is 35 years. 16% are Gen Z; Millennials are 51%; Gen X are 22%; and Baby Boomers are 11%.[8] The dominance of younger generations has implications for capital markets since those individual investors favor ESG investing by purpose-led companies. The evidence to date shows the promising returns of ESG investments, which is why the growth of retail investing is important. Norrsken, discussed in Chapter 1, is an example of an organization that is funding and building new sustainability-based business models, showing early success with portfolio companies, and generating enthusiasm from investors about the viability of sustainable investing.

The investment decisions you and your colleagues make are based on opportunity and risk assessments. When you choose to invest, you do so because the opportunities look promising, and the risks appear manageable. That same logic applies to the shift you make toward ESG-focused decisions. What has changed is that the risks associated with traditional investments once considered reasonable are growing increasingly risky, and opportunities that were once considered risky are now central to your company's survival. Consumer surveys show that people expect companies to be societal stewards of value and will quickly abandon businesses that don't demonstrate greater responsibility. We also know that the financial returns from ESG and adjacent investments are often better than returns for non-ESG companies. Most importantly, we know that we are exceeding the planet's ability to replenish finite resources with our current pace of global demand for "things". The factors shaping what is considered valuable in society are changing right before our eyes and have been doing so for years. The question is not if change is needed, but how quickly you can be part of the solution and not part of the problem.

In 2017 the TCFD (Task Force on Climate-related Financial Disclosures, comprised of leaders from business and industry[9]) published a comprehensive report detailing its recommendations for more robust financial disclosure about the risks and opportunities to the global economy resulting from the climate crisis.[10] At a global macro level, the TCFD report states that transitioning to a lower carbon economy will require approximately $1 trillion in new investments per year.[11] While the price tag seems high, those investments will trigger new innovations and inspire new markets. At a company micro level, these investments represent opportunities and risks to be anticipated in your planning. By explicitly identifying key financial disclosure areas, the TCFD report, summarized below, provides a high-level road map that can help you specify the investment areas best suited for your organization.

## Risks

Transition Risks: *risks related to transitioning "to a lower-carbon economy."*[12] These are:

- *Policy, Legal:* climate-related public policies are evolving, so staying on top of them is vital for your business's survival. It will also help reduce the legal exposure your company might otherwise face for not mitigating damage from your business practices.

- *Technology:* technology advances are accelerating and those will inevitably impact how your company uses energy, deploys, and maintains machinery, requires increased data storage, and more.

- *Market:* there is widespread evidence of changing market needs and beliefs related to the climate crisis, and these will affect the choices people will make.

- *Reputation:* reputation and trust are linked, so if your company is perceived as not demonstrating appropriate sustainability practices, then distrust in your company will erode your reputation.

Transitioning your company to lower carbon status will not be effortless. The investment in planning, money, time, and resources will impact each of the areas above. But the potential long-term gain by aligning your company with the needs of a world struggling to deal with the climate crisis offers significant financial opportunity as well as important moral and societal value benefits.

Physical Risks: *risks from damage incurred by facilities, resources, people due to climate change.*[13] Two physical risks are:

- *Acute:* these are event-driven risks from weather and storms. While you cannot predict storms and their severity over time, you have an obligation to prepare contingencies when catastrophic events occur, first to protect people; and second to minimize physical damage to operations.

- *Chronic:* these are long-term, sustained risks due to climate change. Location will determine the types of disruptions your business might face so plan your sustainability investments accordingly.

The TFCD report is comprehensive and has a framework you can use as a guide for planning the financial impact on your company's income statement, balance sheet, and cash flow statement. You will undoubtedly identify more detailed potential risk and opportunity impacts, so using this will help your company be better prepared for different climate change scenarios. But doing nothing is irresponsible. Ignoring evidence feeds ignorance and will cause you to miss important ways to improve your business strategically in the market and practically in society.

## Opportunities

Existential challenges like the climate crisis can stimulate remarkable ingenuity. Examples:

- The climate crisis has accelerated innovation in renewables while decreasing costs.

- The global pandemic led to the rapid development of the Covid vaccines.

- Aging populations, particularly in western economies, are driving healthcare innovations from telemedicine to remote testing to virtual ICUs.

- Carbon emissions from the world's vehicles (from manufacturing to daily usage) inspired Kevin Czinger's Divergent 3D (Chapter 12) to invent a pathbreaking manufacturing process with enormous potential beyond automobiles.

- The trend of global populations shifting increasingly to urban areas is sparking investment in the smart cities movement.

McKinsey surveyed over 200 companies (2020) to gauge their reaction to the Covid-19 pandemic. Most leaders surveyed (90%) believed that the pandemic will significantly change how business is done in the coming years. The anticipated change is fraught, with 85% of the respondents worried about Covid's impact to their customers and only 21% confident that they have the capability to effectively address the opportunities. At the same time, nearly 75% of them foresee important opportunities arising because of the pandemic.[14] PwC's annual CEO survey (2021) found that 30% of CEOs are "extremely concerned" about climate change. Yet in that same survey, 60% of them have not included any climate-related changes to their plans and investments. Global business involvement and investment is far behind government targets,[15] but the good news is that the EC's and US SEC's efforts to require climate and sustainability disclosures in annual reporting will help catalyze more companies to get involved.

### Increase in Costs from Climate Change to Date

11 of the hottest years on record have occurred since 2005, with 2020 nearly tied with 2016 as the hottest in recorded history.[16] July 2021 was earth's hottest month ever.[17] The costs are enormous – about US$3 trillion since 2010 – which is $1 trillion larger than the prior decade.[18] There were 50 billion-dollar plus climate-related disasters worldwide in 2020 costing nearly $260 billion.[19] In 2020, in the US alone, there were 22 billion-dollar plus climate-related disasters (the largest number ever) causing $95 billion in damages, more than double the average since 1980. Since 1980, the US has experienced 285 billion-dollar disasters costing nearly $1.9 trillion. These costs ultimately affect consumers, markets, and businesses.

### Project Financial Impact from Climate Change by 2050 (from New Climate Economics Index)[20]

A Swiss Re study (2021) highlights the potential impact to the economies of 48 countries (90% of global economy).

- 18% reduction in global GDP if no actions are taken (3.2°C increase)

- 14% reduction if some actions are taken (2.6°C increase)

- 11% reduction if further actions are taken (2°C increase)

- 4% reduction if Paris targets are met (below 2°C increase)

If your company takes no action, then you are contributing to future climate disasters and the corresponding human and financial costs, plus the GDP reductions shown above, certainly not a pride-inducing or defensible survival decision. Yet it is tempting to join those who believe it is impractical to expect companies to make the necessary changes and investments that would help achieve global climate targets. But if you take a moment to consider the physical impacts we're already experiencing, then the transition risks are sensible and morally correct. While it is hard for company leaders to care for the world 30 years in the future, it is hard to ignore the increasing number of climate-related disasters we are experiencing today, from increased wildfires across the world, to more severe hurricanes and tropical storms, to rising seas from melting polar ice caps. Maybe your company is not directly affected yet. But you don't operate in a vacuum, so it is likely many of your suppliers, value chain partners, and customers are directly affected, and it is literally a matter of time before your company is caught sideways if you are not prepared.

## FOCUS AREAS TO HELP FINANCIAL VALUE

### Market Engagement

To get more people on board with caring about crises like climate change, and to involve them in creating better financial value, you must start meeting them and conversing with them in a way that shows you understand where it affects them most. You must step up and reach out to your employees, to your board, to the regulatory bodies shaping new disclosure requirements, to shareholders, to customers, and to the communities where your company works.

### Economic Security

A word of caution. There is no perfect 1:1 transition from the old economy to the new where your company's financial value is magically sustained or increased and where people seamlessly slot into a new job from an old one. Transitions are hard on people, operations, and ecosystem partners. Much of my argument to this point has been to you, the business leader, who likely has a reasonably comfortable position that provides a measure of economic security and status. You understand the intellectual arguments even if you don't agree with every prescription I provide. You have the confidence born from having risen through the management ranks, dealing with internal politics, and making enough good decisions to be considered successful at what you do. But now consider your employees. Some have economic security (not as good as yours, but good enough...), but many don't. Yet you need them on board with the changes you'll be making. You won't get their support if they are paid so little that they must work multiple jobs. In the US, many employees do not have access to insurance. If you push them to work harder, or longer hours, or to make more sacrifices for some unidentified future benefit yet you don't improve their compensation (including benefits) then you won't gain their support. Working multiple jobs just to make ends meet leaves people exhausted, lacking the bandwidth to even be willing to consider climate change (or social justice, or vaccinations...). The moral thing to do is help improve this by improving the compensation packages you offer. It costs more and will change your profitability. But that's the point of the societal value motive. We're not trying to enrich a narrow group of shareholders; we're trying to enrich all stakeholders. That's why the efforts by the EC, SEC, BlackRock, TPG and others are so important: they are pushing us to redefine our definition of success to be more societally focused, not shareholder-driven.

## Your Board of Directors

Helle Bank Jørgensen's Competent Boards is actively filling a knowledge gap to help board members gain fluency about environmental and social crises. Your role as a leader is to be knowledgeable and conversant about the impact to your company from your ESG decisions and to credibly discuss these with your board members so they can advise meaningfully. Better informed boards will be better advisors to senior management.

## Regulatory Bodies

Regulators shape the reporting agenda, and the movement to increase sustainability-related financial disclosures is good for society, even if it is inconvenient to businesses. Trying to lobby against changes, or finding loopholes, doesn't demonstrate a sincere desire to be a positive force for good. Instead, these actions expose you to the wrath of a marketplace that, research shows, wants businesses to be contribute meaningfully to society. Sit down with regulators to show you understand the importance of the work they are doing and explain how your company will support regulatory changes. Remember, we're in this together.

## Shareholders

Shareholders want a return on their investment, so employing a consistent communication strategy that outlines your company's long-term ESG rationale and objectives, supported by evidence, will help. As regulatory changes and more climate disclosures are enacted, shareholders will begin to understand the impact these will have on future firm performance. Shareholder meetings will remain important, with more of them conducted virtually, allowing smaller shareholders (i.e. those retail investors...) an opportunity to participate regularly. You'll lose some old-school shareholders, but will gain shareholders with new perspectives, too.

## Customers

Momentum is in your company's favor to transform into a force for economic and social good. The overwhelming majority of customers (consumers and businesses) worldwide show this in numerous studies. Will you lose some customers because of your changes? Probably. But you don't want those customers ultimately.

## The Climate Activist Community

Too often the activist community views the climate crisis as a pollution argument, not an economic equity issue, defining disadvantaged communities by pollution levels. Local level needs are very different because the impact now on a given population in a specific location from acute events is more relevant because the people in those communities feel and live those issues every day (land use planning, pollution control, setbacks, adaptation, and resilience...). Saying to people "you'll continue to be disadvantaged but you'll have less pollution" won't win them over. Conversely, by working with activists to explain how your changes will reduce pollution *and* create economic opportunity, you may well gain a complementary partner.

## SO WHAT?

Financial value is realized by doing other things well first, specifically focusing on your reputational, organizational, and societal values. The evidence shows the potential for improved revenues, reduced operating/legal and operating costs, as well as the reputation gains and boost employees will feel by being actively involved in supporting your force for good efforts.

Denmark's Ørsted A/S offers a great lesson in financial value gained from massive transformation. It is a vastly different company today than 2009 when fossil fuels generated 85% of its power generation. Today renewable energy generates 85%, and the company has decreased $CO_2$ emissions by 80%. In 2020 Ørsted A/S was ranked the world's most sustainable company.[21] Costs declined nearly 40%. They divested from past core areas, reinvesting the money into their primary focus area of wind energy, and took government subsidies. The transformation was not pain free as operationalizing their plans caused some people to leave, including shareholders and board members.[22] But those that stuck with it benefitted from financial value gains. Ørsted A/S's value has more than doubled the past decade to over $40 billion and their return on capital is nearly 400 basis points higher than the average in Europe. As CEO Henrik Poulsen (who stepped down in early 2021) said "Running the company just for profit doesn't make sense but running it just for a bigger purpose is also not sustainable in the long term. Doing good and doing well must go together."[23]

Kate Gordon said it best: the climate crisis is a big tent opportunity. Ørsted A/S understood this in 2009 and is reaping the benefits today. To enjoy the upside as Ørsted A/S has, you've got to begin mapping out your risks and opportunities today.

## END OF SECTION 2

We've focused on how value is created that, ultimately, leads to financial value. Key section themes:

1. What creates value?
   - Determine how your solution(s) will build and strengthen trust with stakeholders
   - Determine what will rally your employees to support your ambitions

- Determine positive outcomes people will gain wherever your solutions are used
- Determine the economic and financial indicators that will gauge your success

In Section 3 you'll learn how mobilize value to improve your company's contribution to society.

## NOTES

1. Fonny, M. (2020). African proverbs collection 2020: There are no shortcuts to the top of the palm tree. Cover. Retrieved from https://www.amazon.com/African-Proverbs-Collection-2020-Cameroonian/dp/B08MHGFZCJ.
2. Kerber, R. (2021). BlackRock's Fink wants more sustainability data from private cos. Reuters. Retrieved from https://www.reuters.com/business/sustainable-business/blackrocks-fink-wants-more-sustainability-data-private-cos-2021-04-07/.
3. No author. (2021). TPG's impact investing arm taps its $5.5bn Rise Fund to acquire a teacher certification company from PE firm. Private Equity Insights. Retrieved from https://pe-insights.com/news/2021/09/03/tpgs-impact-investing-arm-taps-its-5-5bn-rise-fund-to-acquire-a-teacher-certification-company-from-pe-firm/.
4. Gerber, M. S., Norman, G., & Toms, S. (2021). ESG in 2021 so far: An update. Retrieved from https://corpgov.law.harvard.edu/2021/09/18/esg-in-2021-so-far-an-update/.
5. No author. (2021). European Climate Law. European Commission. Retrieved from https://ec.europa.eu/clima/policies/eu-climate-action/law_en.
6. Quinson, T. (2021). SEC takes a different route than Europe on climate disclosures. Bloomberg. Retrieved from https://www.bloomberg.com/news/articles/2021-09-15/the-sec-is-taking-a-different-route-than-europe-on-climate-disclosures.
7. Hortz, B., & Aferiat, D. (2021). Survey on the 2021 state of the independent retail investor. Retrieved from https://www.nasdaq.com/articles/survey-on-the-2021-state-of-the-independent-retail-investor-2021-05-25.
8. No author. (2020). The rise of the investor generation: Charles Schwab. Retrieved from https://www.aboutschwab.com/generation-investor-study-2021.
9. Some will doubt the TCFD's recommendations on the basis that business and finance leaders are biased and, therefore, we should be skeptical of the recommendations. However, the TCFD is advocating openly for more robust financial disclosures and is open about needing to further improve its recommendations on the precision of climate-related financial disclosures. The TCFD's recommendations are a starting point and, rather than blame the messenger, skeptics should join collaboratively with business leaders, government, NGOs and community actors to share their insights.

10. (2017). TCFD |Task Force on Climate-Related Financial Disclosures. p.V. Retrieved from https://assets.bbhub.io/company/sites/60/2020/10/FINAL-2017-TCFD-Report-11052018.pdf.
11. See footnote 10. p. ii.
12. See footnote 10. p. 5.
13. See footnote 10. p. 6.
14. Bar Am, J., Furstenthal, L., Jorge, F., & Roth, E. (2020). Innovation in a crisis: Why it is more critical than ever. McKinsey. Retrieved from https://www.mckinsey.com/business-functions/strategy-and-corporate-finance/our-insights/innovation-in-a-crisis-why-it-is-more-critical-than-ever.
15. Herbst, S., & Plasschaert, A. (2021). PwC 24th Annual Global CEO Survey-A leadership agenda to take on tomorrow. PwC. Retrieved from https://www.pwc.com/gx/en/ceo-agenda/ceosurvey/2021/report.html.
16. Multiple sources: (1) Thompson, A. (2021). NASA says 2020 tied for hottest year on record. *Scientific American.* Retrieved from https://www.scientific american.com/article/2020-will-rival-2016-for-hottest-year-on-record/. (2). No author. (2020). 10 hottest years on record globally. Climate Central. Retrieved from https://www.climatecentral.org/gallery/graphics/top-10-warmest-years-on-record.
17. No author. (2021). It's official: July was Earth's hottest month on record. Retrieved from https://www.noaa.gov/news/its-official-july-2021-was-earths-hottest-month-on-record.
18. Peterson, E. R., & Laudicina, P. A. (2021). The economic costs of climate change: Lessons learned from COVID-19. Kearney. Retrieved from https://www.kearney.com/web/global-business-policy-council/article/?/a/the-economic-costs-of-climate-change-lessons-learned-from-covid-19.
19. Masters, J. (2021). World hammered by record 50 billion-dollar weather disasters in 2020. Yale Climate Connections. Retrieved from https://yaleclimateconnections.org/2021/01/world-hammered-by-record-50-billion-dollar-weather-disasters-in-2020/.
20. No author. (2021). World economy set to lose up to 18% GDP from climate change if no action taken, reveals Swiss Re Institute's stress-test analysis. Retrieved from https://www.swissre.com/media/news-releases/nr-20210422-economics-of-climate-change-risks.html.
21. Multiple sources: (1) Neubert, M., & Tryggestad, C. (2020). Ørsted's renewable-energy transformation. McKinsey. Retrieved from https://www.mckinsey.com/business-functions/sustainability/our-insights/orsteds-renewable-energy-transformation. (2) Scott, M. (2020). Top company profile: Denmark's Ørsted is 2020's most sustainable corporation. Retrieved from https://www.corporateknights.com/reports/2020-global-100/top-company-profile-orsted-sustainability-15795648/.
22. McFarlane, S. (2021). One oil company's rocky path to renewable energy. *The Wall Street Journal.* Retrieved from https://www.wsj.com/articles/one-oil-companys-rocky-path-to-renewable-energy-orsted-11623170953.
23. See footnote 22.

# Section 3

# VALUE MOBILIZATION

# 9

# CULTIVATING STAKEHOLDERS

*The most valuable service is one rendered to our fellow humans.*[1]
—*Buddhist Maxim*

"Companies have historically felt safest on the solid ground of being 'neutral' when it comes to sensitive issues involving people and planet. This is not a surprising situation given leaders would prefer not to risk alienating potentially large numbers of customers. This is the transactional dimension taking priority. Brave souls that want to be a positive social force like Marc Beniof are few and far between. Marc is not afraid to do or say what needs to be done or said, and I would argue his influence has only grown as a result. Yet we need many more CEOs and senior leaders to 'step forward' if businesses are to become much more of a positive engine," says Steve Leonard, CEO of Singularity University. A seasoned senior executive in the technology industry who has lived and worked all over the world, Steve has been part of forming many deep-tech startups and led multi-billion-dollar divisions of public companies. He has spoken at many global events and conferences, including the United Nations Development Program and United Nations Economic and Social Commission for Asia. He is clear in his view about getting businesses to change into a durable and persistent force for good-it's unlikely until more leaders with confidence and conviction step up. Even then courageous leadership may not be enough. As he says, inertia is a powerful reality. Starting something takes effort and so does stopping something, so it is easy to stay channelled within a narrow range of comfortable practices. Leaders may say being a more engaged societal participant is important but when push comes to shove a business leader will simply ask 'will shareholders reward me?' Boards, too, are creatures of the system they oversee and will be reluctant to encourage the senior leaders to take bold actions toward positive societal value because they too value risk avoidance when the rewards of constructive disruption are uncertain and hard to manage once begun. Furthermore, there is the usual eye rolling cynicism among many company leaders that view ESG as simply the latest trend and, sadly, some will jump on the bandwagon because of this, then jump off when society moves onto the next hot topic. Plus, the complexity of rearchitecting a company's entire supply chain cannot be overstated. Agreements between ecosystem partners are filled with legalese and performance parameters that strictly guide how businesses within can maneuver. It comes down to a simple truism: businesses today exist to manifest growth that ultimately rewards shareholders. As stark as this sounds, Steve is an optimist. He's seen change happen before. He's led impactful change initiatives himself, including important work he did as Founding CEO of SGInnovate in Singapore, an organization focused on creating a new generation of deep technology companies. He built a team that, coupled with scientific research, worked with a diverse range of stakeholders locally and internationally, including venture capitalists, global companies, and leading universities, to spawn innovative early-stage companies. Within just a couple of years 90 start-ups were built and a community of 33,000 + members was formed. In addition to his business accomplishments Steve has been actively involved in farm-field irrigation systems in Cambodia for more than 20 years. For all his work with exponential technology and those who are building the future, he takes pains to recognise the field irrigation as more about exponential impact. Simple, low-cost technology applied in useful ways that have increased crop yields and associated incomes for farmers by 10X in some areas. Whatever venture Steve is pursuing, he focuses on a few key questions:

- Is this a problem of convenience or a problem of importance? Plenty of people are working on problems of convenience (speedier grocery deliver to your door for example) as compared to improving drought-resistant crops or reducing food-packaging waste, which he would categorise as 'important'.

- Who are the people that have the capability and interest in working on this problem over time? Many people are interested but not capable and many people are capable but not interested. How do we attract those people who are both...?

- If we can successfully tackle this problem, will it improve the lives of billions of people in some way?

These questions are just as applicable to the converging crises we now face worldwide. And as Steve says, for meaningful change to occur that inspires businesses to become a collective force for good there needs to be an exogenous, forcing function, such as government regulations or major business influencers. The Covid vaccines are an example of this. Driven by a shared interest in helping people by addressing the pandemic, governments not only made finding a vaccine a priority but worked with large pharmaceutical companies to focus their R&D efforts on this. Then, once the vaccines were developed those same institutions, plus a wide range of providers from business to NGOs to armed forces to community groups, worked together on logistics and distribution. Steve's earlier point about businesses being transactional is one of the obstacles to getting consistent participation from them to help with the climate crisis. Or economic inequality. Or social injustice. The pandemic was a visceral, tangible threat that people could understand, particularly because the consequences of inaction were known to be horrible. There was a moral responsibility for different societal groups to collaborate. The impediment in the way of galvanizing collective action from multiple stakeholders to help solve these other crises is determining how to show these are just as tangible and threatening, even though not everyone experiences them the same way. Even with a significant influencer, success is unlikely unless different stakeholders come together. Therein lies the challenge. Even with the abundance of evidence about the climate crisis, and social injustice, and economic inequality many people see these as abstract, distant events that don't impact them daily. And the ultimate irony is that the climate crisis impacts everything we do. It's the obvious problem right in front of our faces, but we don't see it because it is everywhere all the time, so it is now part of our everyday existence. Climate affects pollution levels worldwide and hits disadvantaged communities the hardest. Climate changes environmental ecosystems, which affects the food supply, and plants with medicinal properties, and weather, and fresh water. The chain of impacts is long.

## IT'S ABOUT YOUR STAKEHOLDERS

It's blindingly obvious that the world today is vastly different than when most of today's companies were founded. We've discussed the signals earlier: consumers want companies to do good; ESG and sustainable investment approaches show better returns; scientific evidence says earth is baking because of human activity, driven primarily by industrial practices; economic inequality is worsening; pandemics spread easily; misinformation is more prevalent than ever. No company can continue to operate as if it were yesterday using century old models, especially the profit motive that has increasingly distorted what companies and their leaders define as successful. Business is not here just to enrich shareholders. Businesses employee people, innovate solutions, collaborate with governments, engage in local communities...yet we treat these roles as subservient to shareholders. Your role as a leader in your company is not separate from your role as a participant in your local community or in society at large. Therefore, you need to collaborate forthrightly with the broader array of stakeholders because, at the end of the day, we're all in this together. As Benjamin Franklin famously said "we must, indeed, all hang together or, most assuredly, we will all hang separately."

Eighty-seven percent of people see stakeholders as crucial to success[2] so your stakeholder strategy must have a 'what all parties will gain' outcome. Productive stakeholder relationships result from thoughtful outreach by you to them to create a community of shared interests. Doing so will improve the potential for them to become advocates for you and you for them. Not every stakeholder relationship is going to have perfect symmetry among these interests, but if you begin by understanding mutual outcomes as a common need then you will have created a compass heading for evaluating the long-term value created from your relationship.

Salesforce.com Founder Marc Beniof established uncompromising expectations for himself, the company, and the entire stakeholder community: he is unequivocal in wanting Salesforce to make the world better. He has been an outspoken proponent of stakeholder engagement since its founding. At inception he created the "1/1/1 model" in which each office devotes 1% of profits, 1% of equity, and 1% of employee time to the local community, which has amounted to $240 million in grants, 3.5 million hours of community service, and products to nearly 40,000 non-profits.[3] Salesforce is a fierce advocate for social issues, including full support for LGBTQ rights. Beniof reinforces diversity everyday knowing that employees "want to work for a company that has a meaning associated with it, not just a product." Each year the company produces its annual Stakeholder Impact Report, a detailed review of its stakeholder initiatives, investments, and impact. FY21's highlights include:[4]

1. Partner ecosystem: the company has over 350 partners worldwide

2. Environmental impact: Salesforce funded 10 million trees and aims to fund 100 million trees by 2030 as part of the World Economic Forum's Trillion Trees Challenge

3. Education: invested $120 million globally to support high quality education

4. Social justice:
   - $100 million invested in Black-owned businesses by 2023 and will increase by 25% per year
   - $200 million committed to benefit racial equity and justice

5. Covid-19 response:
   - Sourced 50 million PPE units for first responders
   - Donated $7 million to support small businesses

6. Societal value: delivered $1.5 billion in social value in FY21

7. The company also reports the following about its diversity, equity, and inclusion efforts:
   - 47.4% of the company's workforce is comprised of diverse groups (LGBTQ, Women, Black, Latinx, Indigenous, Disabilities, Veterans) with the goal of achieving 50% by 2023.[5]

8. Salesforce's leadership team is 29.4% gender diverse;[6]

9. Thirty-six of Salesforce's board is gender and ethnically diverse;[7]

10. The company has been closing the gender pay gap, with $3.8 million spent in 2021 and $16.2 million since 2015 to fix unexplained pay differences.[8]

Beniof walks the talk with customers by meeting with them directly, listening to them, and improving Salesforce's offerings based on their direct input. He set expectations that ecosystem partners should have similar social values to Salesforce's. With encouragement from Colin Powell, a member of Salesforce's Board of Directors and former US Secretary of State who passed away in October 2021, Beniof embedded philanthropy into Salesforce's business practices from the beginning. As he says *"I default to this concept of stakeholder theory. CEOs have to decide: are they advocating for their shareholders or advocating for their stakeholders? If you're only focused on shareholders, then you've got a very different situation on your hands. And in our case, we are very much focused on stakeholder theory."*[9]

The time has long past when companies wielded control over stakeholders. Stakeholders have the upper-hand and their influence drives the fate of companies. That means businesses must be more engaged with the needs of society wherever they operate. Not just to sell their wares but to be an active participant in the communities they serve.

## Stakeholders and the Forcing Event

While economic prosperity and total wealth have increased for the past century, the spoils have been unevenly distributed, with the rich getting richer whereas working wages have been stagnant. Furthermore, economic gains came at a cost to our environment. Plus, structural barriers have been erected over the decades across countries that have favored a few select stakeholders over others. Unless there is a credible forcing event that compels businesses everywhere to change, uneven advances in company-initiated ESG investments will continue. There are some good signs. In 2021 136 countries agreed to a minimum global corporate tax rate of 15%, with the intent to stop the use of tax havens.[10] The proposed tax may well become the kind of a forcing event the world needs. Courageous company leaders don't have to wait for finalized global action from more governments. They can make the moral, ethical, and strategic investment decisions today to start rectifying the imbalances and improve outcomes for more stakeholders.

What do you *really* understand about your stakeholders? If you are completely honest then you'll know that the profit motive has focused business attention on enriching shareholders. We also know that customer stakeholders, for example, are often treated as a statistical sea of abstract purchasers with generic characteristics whose support increases our market share and financial results, including share price and dividends, benefitting shareholders. Furthermore, we know that large companies exert outsized pressure on smaller supply chain stakeholders to reduce prices, which improves the larger company's bottom line, boosts share price, and enriches shareholders. Most companies are operating honorably within accepted standards. But there are also outliers that game the system to juice financial results to achieve a short-term gain. Gaming the system has helped drive skyrocketing CEO pay. In the 1950s CEOs earned 20 times more than the average employee; by 2018 CEOs earned 361 times more than employees. CEO pay has grown 1000% since then, whereas wages for average workers have been mostly stagnant.[11] During the pandemic we've seen government funding in the US to help workers be redirected by many companies to pay for share buybacks that boosted stock prices, rewarding shareholders and senior executives holding options. There is a growing backlash from the public over egregious CEO pay and, in the US in particular, legislation is being considered to curb the escalating compensation packages. Efforts in the U.S. Congress are underway to refocus on anti-trust, directed particularly toward a handful of big tech companies[12] that have allowed false information on their platforms, spurring a post-truth mentality in some pockets of society leading to destructive consequences, notably the January 6, 2021, insurrection in Washington D.C. That's hardly admirable behavior by these companies as far as employee stakeholders and societal goodwill are concerned. This maelstrom of events is the by-product of systemic social and economic structures that reward a few and penalize many more.

To meet stakeholders where they are follow the Stakeholder Involvement Steps (SIS) here:

1. Deepen your stakeholder insights

2. Identify compelling reasons

3. Invite employee input

4. Ensure alignment

5. Determine business model changes

6. Take action

7. Report results

Each of the Stakeholder Involvement Steps have economic, political, and social dimensions (note that your work is presumed to help improve the environment, whether that is planetary, societal, or economic health). Think of them as twenty-first century EPS (not earnings per share, but expectations per stakeholder):

- *Economic:* what will each stakeholder gain financially from the relationship; and

- *Political:* will we be viewed favorably by others as an outgrowth of this relationship; and

- *Social:* how will our combined collaborative actions improve societal outcomes for the communities we serve.

## Stakeholder Involvement Steps

SIP guides you in thinking through the stakeholders in your ecosystem and which ones you need to help your company achieve its aspiration. Both internal and external stakeholders matter. Internal includes all employees, shareholders, boards. External includes customers, value chain partners, community groups, and government actors.

1. Deepen your stakeholder insights
   Invest in understanding your stakeholders' motivations and challenges.
   *Economic:* Gather qualitative and quantitative data from your stakeholders about where their economic interest lies and the relationship to your aspiration. Your conversations with them will reveal which stakeholders are the best fit for your transformation.

   *Political:* Be attentive to your stakeholders' respective reputations and how being part of your transformation can enhance their credibility.

Remember, you want stakeholders who share your desire to do what is right and be inspired to introduce you to other key influencers they know who might help.

*Social:* Part of your effort at this stage is for you to describe why that stakeholder is important to your plans and how the combination of you and them strengthens your ability to create meaningful and measurable value for the communities you collectively serve.

2. Identify compelling reasons
   Identify factors that will help persuade stakeholders to become champions for your company, including any hot buttons that are their personal calls to action. Decode your stakeholders' interests in and motivations for creating force for good value.

   *Economic:* Provide credible evidence that supports your aspiration. Be transparent about the potential long-term economic consequences, and why supporting you makes the whole greater than the sum of the parts. Stakeholders want to know that you understand the capabilities you have and that you believe are required to fulfill you ambitions, and that you will seek their input as conditions dictate.

   *Political:* Value arises when you show how your efforts combined with theirs can help them gain credibility for being responsible. Just as you need and want access to your stakeholders' networks let them know how your network of influencers can help them.

   *Social:* Show where your interests and those of your stakeholder address wellbeing and quality of life. Work with your stakeholders to identify and articulate a common set of benefits your combined efforts would create for your communities and, of course, how their collaboration can endear them to the local community.

3. Invite employee input
   Invest in understanding your employees' own expertise and invite them to become active contributors.

   *Economic:* Just as you share your company's projections for the future, be clear with employees about the rationale for the changes you are making and the corresponding impacts on performance in both the short and long term. Furthermore, outline how the changes may benefit them, even though those benefits are likely to be 2–3 years later.

*Political:* Work with your employees on strengthening their intra and inter-company professional networks. This will help connect them to other influential people and build their own internal political capital. Build this into your people development actions in support of your transformation.

*Social:* Being a force for good means encouraging employees to seek ways to be involved in society wherever they are located. Ask for their recommendations on how to best serve local communities.

4. Ensure alignment

    Ensure your stakeholders are aligned with your aspiration. That's more than just your shareholders. Your Board, employees, customers, ecosystem partners, community groups, government agencies, regulatory bodies, and NGOs, are included, too.

    *Economic:* Ensure financial and economic interests are aligned with agreed upon principles to guide periodic reviews. Alignment reduces friction in the relationship that would otherwise arise when stakeholder interests diverge.

    *Political:* Agree to the potential marketplace reputation benefits to be gained from aligning with your stakeholders. Stakeholder alignment can lead to real consequences for improving society, serving as a persuasive, uplifting signal that you are doing this to collectively address complex challenges.

    *Social:* Be clear that your ambitions are aligned with the community's life interests and are not some temporary feel-good PR stunt. Stakeholder alignment signals to the community a collective effort to be a force for good.

5. Determine business model changes

    Transformation is about co-creating a business model with your stakeholders that supports growing positive societal value. Define the rules of conduct expected of each stakeholder. Understand stakeholder interdependencies as that will help you understand each of their respective expertise, identifies where gaps exist in the ecosystem, and strengthens your combined financial capabilities for optimizing societal value.

*Economic:* You must paint a picture for how the entire ecosystem you are proposing creates measurable value that each partner will share because of a more collaborative business model. Highlight where you think the long-term gains will come, that short term pains are likely, and how to communicate those to the communities you serve.

*Political:* You, and each of your stakeholders, will probably discover political consequences from the changes you are proposing. Map these out as there will be knock-on effects that affect professional relationships and partnerships.

*Social:* Your relationships with the people in the communities you serve will be impacted by your business model changes so you'll need to show how your changes will ultimately be good for them while also working with your ecosystem partners to clearly identify weaknesses in your business model that could upset other stakeholders. You won't have 100% flawless execution or unanimous support from your communities. But the changes made toward becoming a collective force for good are likely to earn more supporters than you lose.

6. Take action

The first five steps articulate key elements of your strategic rationale for building a stronger stakeholder community. Now plan the specific implementation actions you must pursue to build a networked stakeholder community of shared interest around your force for good aspiration. Work with ecosystem partners to develop a communication plan explaining how messaging will be deployed to the market, including digital.

*Economic:* Businesses regularly project their financial performance for the future. You'll do the same here. Think in practical, executable terms for the next 1–3 years first. Longer-term projections beyond 3 years too often lead to unrealistic goals. Demonstrating progress and celebrating even small wins are vital in building confidence. Track data and transparently share with stakeholders. Map out the projected change milestones and the periodic in-process reviews for all stakeholders, including who will take the lead on any adjustments to the plan as the implementation evolves.

*Political:* Understand any regulatory actions that may be coming. Remember Steve Leonard's point that forcing functions galvanize large-scale action, and governments are often the largest of these.

*Social:* Focus on direct outreach designed to inspire community groups, describing why you are doing what you are doing, how you will be working as a collaborative stakeholder system, that things may not always be perfect but that you will be open and transparent about what is working, what you are learning, and how it is benefitting them.

7. Reporting results
Building on point 6, get ahead of the regulatory changes. In 2018 the European Commission (EC) outlined sustainability measures for companies. In 2021 all 27 EC members committed to reduce emissions 55% by 2030, based on 1990 levels.[13] Also in 2021 the U.S.'s Securities and Exchange Commission, led by Gary Gensler, was developing mandatory climate risk disclosure rules.[14] These actions will have a direct impact on other markets ultimately, so tracking your disclosure data now is smart.

*Economic:* New reporting requirements will impose new costs on your company because you will have to prepare more detailed business reviews. Start incorporating this data now, even if it is incomplete or the reporting requirements are opaque.

*Political:* Get in touch with your regulatory agencies and elected officials. This is not to suggest you lobby regulators to favor your company and ease reporting burdens. Those burdens are coming. Instead, build a relationship because you want to demonstrate you are eager to be a good, and responsible, corporate citizen. You don't want to run afoul of their requirements because you didn't take the time to understand the changes or get to know the people enacting them.

*Social:* You're transforming into a force for good because you want to be a reliable and trusted community partner, so report your results to them and host forums to gain community feedback. You won't always agree with each other, but the effort to listen and acknowledge community input will go a long way toward strengthening your reputation.

To illustrate, The Chicago Community Trust (TCCT) is a community foundation focused on reducing "racial and ethnic wealth inequity."[15] Chicago ranks 50th of the 50 largest US cities for having poor upward opportunities, and related racial disparities, for black versus white men. Sixty-five percent of Latinx and Black households are in dire financial straits and can survive above the poverty line for only three months if their income disappeared. That compares to 28% of white households. More than $4.4 billion could be generated annually within the region if disparities were eliminated, plus GDP would increase $8 billion.[16] TCCT's stakeholders? Citizens, investors, funding organizations, neighborhood groups, and local leaders in business and government. TCCT knows and understands them. TCCT has existed for 100 years and has built relationships with community members based on knowing the various societal groups that are interested in making the region better balanced economically. TCCT's stakeholders have a shared interest in a more prosperous Chicago with reduced racial and ethnic wealth inequity. This will also help solve adjacent issues like improving health, reducing violence, and strengthening education. In 2019 TCCT sharpened its focus specifically around fixing racial and ethnic wealth inequities. Recasting its strategy understandably altered how TCCT identifies with and relates to stakeholders. Similarly, your business model and stakeholder relationships are likely to change because the needs of society have changed.

## So What?

Show you are as invested in local communities as you expect them to be in you. It's not a zero-sum game. You and your stakeholders will each gain more by working together on shared interests. Your value chain partners, for example, may have been selected for pricing considerations but if their operating practices don't tick the 'force-for-good transformation boxes' then negotiate a partnership exit. Look, part of your company's success in a world needing innovative ways to address today's converging crises relies on having a more accurate understanding of your stakeholders than you had in the past.

The logic of knowing your stakeholders better isn't hard to grasp. Better data leads to better understanding which leads to better decisions. Note that I am not saying 'more data' as volumes of data can lead to confusion. Better data is the result of having a blueprint that identifies what society needs, integrates it with your aspiration, asks key stakeholders within what they hope and expect your company can provide to address those needs, and what capabilities you have and will need to create meaningful societal value. Steve Leonard reminds us that businesses are transactional. Given this, your task is determining how to be more relational in pursuit of societal value creation. Marc Beniof and Salesforce created the 1/1/1 model to help guide their stakeholders and enhance the company's societal contribution. TCCT is driven to fix racial and wealth inequities for their stakeholders. Determine where value resides for you and your stakeholders, then co-create a plan for developing it. Transformation is not just about how to make money but how to create positive societal value. Chapter 10 will show you how to find those interdependencies among stakeholders so that you can collectively pursue societal value creation.

## NOTES

1. Staff Contributor. (2017). Buddha reveals 9 golden rules to achieving your goals and living the life you want. BBN. Retrieved from https://www.bbncommunity.com/buddha-reveals-9-golden-rules-achieving-goals-living-life-want/.
2. Greene, M. (2020). Let's get concrete about stakeholder capitalism. Harvard Law Forum on Corporate Governance. Retrieved from https://corpgov.law.harvard.edu/2020/02/12/lets-get-concrete-about-stakeholder-capitalism/.
3. No author. No date. 1% Model. Salesforce.com. Retrieved from https://www.salesforce.org/pledge-1/.
4. No author. (2021). FY21 Stakeholder impact report. Retrieved from https://stakeholderimpactreport.salesforce.com.
5. No author. No date. Building a workplace that reflects society. Salesforce.com. Retrieved from https://www.salesforce.com/company/equality/.
6. Bradley-Smith, A. (2021). The most gender diverse executive teams in tech in 2021. TheOrg.com. Retrieved from https://theorg.com/insights/the-most-gender-diverse-executive-teams-in-tech-in-2021.
7. No author. No date. Salesforce leadership. Salesforce.com. Retrieved from https://www.salesforce.com/company/leadership/.
8. See footnote 7, 2021 Saleforce Equal Pay Update. Salesforce.com. Retrieved from https://www.salesforce.com/company/equality/.

9. Steinmetz, K. (2016). Salesforce CEO Marc Benioff: 'Anti-LGBT' Bills Are 'Anti-Business'. *Time Magazine*. Retrieved from https://time.com/4276603/marc-benioff-salesforce-lgbt-rfra/.

10. Thomas, L. (2021). 136 countries have agreed to a global minimum tax rate. Here's what it means. *World Economic Forum*. Retrieved from https://www.weforum.org/agenda/2021/11/global-minimum-tax-rate-deal-signed-countries/.

11. Multiple sources: (1) Hembree, D. CEO pay skyrockets to 361 times that of the average worker. (2018). Forbes. Retrieved from https://www.forbes.com/sites/dianahembree/2018/05/22/ceo-pay-skyrockets-to-361-times-that-of-the-average-worker/?sh=1b3177cd776d. (2) Desilver, D. (2018). For most U.S. workers, real wages have barely budged in decades. Pew Research Center. Retrieved from https://www.pewresearch.org/fact-tank/2018/08/07/for-most-us-workers-real-wages-have-barely-budged-for-decades/.

12. McCabe, D., & Lohr, S. (2021). Congress faces renewed pressure to 'modernize our antitrust laws'. Retrieved from https://www.nytimes.com/2021/06/29/technology/facebook-google-antitrust-tech.html.

13. No author. (2021). Delivering the European Green Deal. Retrieved from https://ec.europa.eu/info/strategy/priorities-2019-2024/european-green-deal/delivering-european-green-deal_en.

14. Gensler, G. (2021). Prepared remarks before the principles for responsible investment "climate and global financial markets" webinar. Retrieved from https://www.sec.gov/news/speech/gensler-pri-2021-07-28.

15. No author. (2021). The Chicago Community Trust. About page. Retrieved from https://www.cct.org/about/.

16. See footnote 15. Our strategic plan page. Retrieved from https://www.cct.org/about/strategic-plan/.

# 10

# STIMULATING ENGAGEMENT

*This is shown by being cheerful with them; doing good things for them; serving them; never acting as if superior to them...[1]*
                                                            *–Nana Asma'u*

Mr. Roongrote Rangsiyopash has been the president and CEO of SCG (Siam Cement Group) since 2016. SCG is a century-old, widely respected, multi-billion-dollar regional cement-building materials, packaging and chemicals maker, a capital-intensive business requiring heavy equipment for raw material extraction and processing. Referred to as Khun Roongrote (Khun is an honorific used when referring to either men or women in Thailand), he is a Harvard MBA who joined the company in 1987. Trained as an engineer and business person, before becoming CEO he was President of SCG Paper (now known as SCG Packaging) and Executive Vice President, The Siam Cement PLC. He is a refreshing CEO. Respectful and thoughtful, he is one of those people that when he speaks, people stop to listen. He has the same pressures as any other public CEO: ensure the company's revenues and profits keep growing. Shareholders expect the same. Early on in his CEO tenure he was clear that SCG needed to find ways to modernize and prepare for a very different world than it had operated in for its first century. He was determined that this modernization include becoming more digitally savvy, more entrepreneurial, more sustainable; a set of capabilities that represented a significant operating and cultural shift for a company that had built its reputation from complex engineering projects with long-term investment and payback timeframes. Shortly after he became CEO, I witnessed a townhall-like session he had with managers where he described his rationale for focusing on those new capabilities. One questioner asked him why the qualities he outlined are so important given that SCG didn't depend on those capabilities for its success up to that point. Khun Roongrote answered "I am not entirely sure what the outcome for us will be, but I do know that they are important and that our future depends on our ability to adapt to changing times. What made us successful to this point is not necessarily what will help us stay successful in the future…" Since then, SCG has invested in developing the new capabilities as well as working to reduce greenhouse gas emissions to achieve Paris accord targets (including banning all plastic water bottles from company facilities virtually overnight), to connecting more directly with local communities. As CEO, he engages with a diverse range of stakeholders to learn their interests and gain their support.

When the Covid-19 pandemic hit Khun Roongrote saw two options: focus on the wellbeing of the business; or the wellbeing of employees and their families; both are important. He had to choose one-he chose the latter. Some colleagues and advisors were skeptical because they viewed their responsibility was to shareholders. But Khun Roongrote believed that putting people first was something SCG *had* to do. As he said,

> On the personal level, I had to think not just about profit and growth, but what we could do to make society better. Covid-19 was a crisis and the best thing we could do was to act, explaining why we were acting that way. I thought 'this is what we should reasonably expect of each other; that helping was the way normal people should behave.

SCG's normal operations stopped during Covid-19, so leadership decided to manufacture and help distribute masks, especially for children in remote locations. The company worked with the Foundation for Good Governance on Medicine for a project called "Thai Kids Fight COVID." More than 100,000 masks were provided to children in hard-to-reach locales. Unlike standard medical colors, SCG's masks came in vibrant colors that were appealing to kids. The partnership also created an art competition with messages about healthcare and hygiene. SCG helped develop testing facilities for Thailand, both mobile and embedded, delivering to 20 hospitals in 2 weeks and another 40 hospitals shortly thereafter. They did this is because they have competitive advantages and the operational excellence capabilities, including the knowhow to produce high volumes faster than other organizations. Their unique knowhow helped save Thailand's medical professionals. They coordinated with other leaders on a government commission to track and manage the country's inventory of ventilators, and they used their manufacturing expertise to build new ventilators, plus set up a ventilator repair center. Khun Roongrote reached out to Oxford University and Astra

Zeneca who were working on vaccine development. They were curious; "You're a cement company. Why are you interested in vaccines?". His reply? "I'm not exactly sure, but all I know is that as a citizen of Thailand the best way to get out of the pandemic is to have vaccines, so I want us to help. And at no profit." An SCG sister company became a contract manufacturer for the vaccine. While Covid-19 was raging students in Thailand were staging protests demanding changes in the constitution, political leadership and, most controversially, the monarchy. Khun Roongrote said it was important for SCG to engage with the young generation because they represent Thailand's future. While the company can't recruit 10,000 new employees every year, he believes it must demonstrate societal value by giving the younger generation more meaningful opportunities. The company offers 20,000 scholarships each year to help with their education. It created the Sustainable Development Symposium a decade ago, training younger generations about environment and society, not conflict and violence. Their 2020 edition focused on the circular economy. SCG sponsored Youth-In-Charge, an open integrative platform for youth in Thailand to engage constructively with leaders and decision-makers on various agendas, particularly around advancing the UN SDGs (United Nations Sustainability Development Goals).

Skeptics saw the merits of SCG's genuine concern for the public good and quickly turned into supporters. As Khun Roongrate said, *Do right because it's what you believe, not because it is what you have to do*. SCG created a new sense of meaning by redefining success during COVID not as a fiduciary task to reduce costs, but as a human effort to do what is right for society and, given its history of engagement in the region, strengthened its reputation as a trusted company.[2]

Engaging with stakeholders directly and enthusiastically so they become active advocates for your company is not about advertising to customers, especially in the era of social media. Stakeholders want firms to understand them, not pander to them. What works effectively are company-stakeholder dialogues because they convey that you are taking the time to listen and understand. Furthermore, it helps build a sense of community with shared values. Nurturing stakeholder advocacy has greater potential for positive impact versus the use of advertising methods since the latter is distrusted. Nurturing is not "selling" or "compelling" stakeholders to do something since that suggests aggressive, even manipulative, recruitment. In contrast, nurturing evokes a sense of care and responsibility, qualities that companies need today.

For decades marketing principles as taught in business schools have changed little. For example, STP (segment, target, position) guides marketing planning by prioritizing customer groups, distilling them into common statistical characteristics, then developing advertising messages designed to motivate them to buy your company's offerings. STP is insufficient for today's companies because the framework lacks nuanced insights about customers, and stakeholders overall. The model was developed in an era when digital and social media didn't exist, enabling companies to more easily control customer perceptions. Identifiable brands were built through broadcast TV, radio, and print that concentrated repetitive advertising over a limited array of consumable media. Environmental concerns, social injustice, and growing economic inequality weren't mainstream. Now that we know better, we also need a better approach. CAM is STP's successor.

## STAKEHOLDER MOTIVATION ANALYSIS: CAM (CAUSE, ADVOCACY, MEANING)[3]

CAM is a more effective framework for identifying stakeholders', their motivations, and where societal value resides:

| STP[a] (One-Way Communication) | Purpose | CAM[b] (Dialogue) | Purpose |
|---|---|---|---|
| Segmentation | Identify common characteristics of each market segment (age, income, education...) | Cause | Identifies beliefs, things that are important to them (health, safety, learning...) |
| Targeting | Evaluate attractiveness of segment(s) | Advocacy | Evaluate motivations that will make them your champions |
| Positioning | Create marketing mix relevant to each segment | Meaning | Create connection between what stakeholders value and what they spend time doing |

[a]Kotler, P. (1999). Kotler on marketing: How to create, win and dominate markets. Chapter 6 Designing the Marketing Mix. New York, NY: The Free Press.
[b]John A. Davis. Research 2000–2021.

## CAUSE

Think of Cause as the customer's personal aim, belief or need for which they are seeking a solution, personal validation, and social affinity. When you're at a social gathering you are unlikely to ask people their age, income, or religion (unless you want a quick exit). It's more likely you'll discuss leisure or work experiences and maybe minor personal frustrations. Over time you'll get to know what fuels their raison d'etre. Engaging directly with your stakeholders sheds light on their *cause*, and whether their interests align with your company's. Think about your company's aspiration and then determine the kinds of questions you need answered when engaging with your stakeholders. Shaping your market research around understanding stakeholder *cause* yields richer and more meaningful insights not gathered from conventional marketing approaches. For example, it's impossible to divine accurate personal insights when categorizing people by age group. You can guess based on stereotypes, or your own expertise, or projecting your own views onto other populations but doing so can lead to inaccurate conclusions.[4]

There are two categories of *cause*: little "c" and big "c." Little c is more personal and individual: I have an aim (how can I reduce my energy consumption) so if your company helps in this area, I will be grateful (by becoming a customer or even just an advocate for your business). Big C encompasses societal needs: we have a systemic problem that is incredibly complex (how can we eliminate structural bias in mortgage lending to help address wealth and income inequality), so if your company institutes fair and transparent lending practices, then you'll gain the support of stakeholders like me. In the United States, for example, social inequality and racist practices are embedded in society, as they have been for 400 years as shown via judicial bias, wealth creation and income inequality, healthcare access, and police practices.[5] That does not mean all people are racist. It does mean that there are significant structural inequities plaguing civic relations, inhibiting access to economic, health, and education opportunities. The murders of three black Americans, George Floyd, Breonna Taylor, and Ahmaud Arbery in 2020 catalyzed nationwide protests, reenergized the Black Lives Matter movement, and reignited national interest in how to dismantle the systemic obstacles impeding social progress.[6] Unfortunately, this has become a highly partisan issue between purveyors of fact armed with evidence about redlining, a practice begun in the 1930s that marked neighborhoods as high risk based mostly on their racial makeup and resulted in unfair and predatory lending practices,[7] versus agents of fiction making false claims that election fraud in the 2020 US Presidential election,[8] then using them to justify enacting stricter state-level voting laws that are actually efforts to supress minority voters.[9]

Conducting research to unearth little c and big C causes will give your business richer stakeholder insights that will inspire new thinking for addressing vital needs. Companies can't sit on society's side-lines any longer. Use market research to understand the underlying issues energizing communities in society. As evidence shows, ESG investments have produced higher returns that non-ESG ones. If your aspiration is helping solve social injustice then ingrain Diversity, Equity, and Inclusion into your strategic planning. If your aspiration is to reduce your carbon footprint through 3D manufacturing (See Chapter 12 and Kevin Czinger's company Divergent 3D), then work with your value chain partners to design a new model of manufacturing. You don't have to have a fully baked solution before starting. Questioning convention and inviting new ideas can illuminate the path ahead for effective stakeholder engagement. Plus, you'll be creating great experiences for your stakeholders and setting the tone for other companies.

## ADVOCACY

*Advocacy* is about cultivating stakeholders to become champions for the greater value your company offers society beyond the products and services you sell, and they take on this role because they fundamentally believe in the company, sharing this belief with others. Proponents of design thinking and human-centered design (HCD) encourage businesses to uncover insights about stakeholder behaviors, their "jobs to be done"[10], and even identify latent needs to translate a stakeholder's *cause* into ongoing advocacy. Doing so develops more passionate, fervent, and dedicated stakeholders, akin to how sports organizations foster a community of rabid fans.

Today's economic incentives are stacked against meaningful, systemic change from businesses. But that's partly because business education, decades of global practice, and forgiving regulatory environments have defined success narrowly as *reduce costs, maximize profits*. Other than guilt-driven reasons, businesses won't naturally gravitate to a more socially responsible model. Furthermore, most shareholders and investors are products of a system focused first on increasing their wealth. To accomplish this, shortcuts in understanding customers are made, which is why businesses distil customers into generalizable groups enabling a scalable, volume-driven business model and relegating them to financial data points that eliminates any sense of humanity. If you feel like you're treated as a number, that's because you are. It's a great model from a financial maximization standpoint and a lousy way to treat people if your aspiration is to help improve society.

Focusing on advocacy is the antidote to sterile customer development. But what, exactly, is an advocate? Advocates are stakeholders willing to vouch for your company, its reputation, its products and services, its societal engagement. You don't pay them. And while they may buy the things you sell and therefore represent commercial gain, their belief in your company is what really inspires their enthusiasm for championing the societal value your company represents. This is analogous to how sports clubs foster a community of fans – the clubs aren't just selling them tickets or merchandise – they're connecting fans to the dream that their team *could* win the championship with their support. That deepens people's connection far more than just selling stuff.

Patagonia's stakeholders are a global community of brand advocates. Rather than just sell products, the company sells responsibility. Founder Yvon Chouinard's passion for the outdoors has grown into a global movement advocating that people be stewards of sustainable value and should pay it forward to others so they, too, can enjoy nature. Patagonia's stakeholders understand that the company's aspiration is rooted in environmental responsibility, not making money, even though it is financially successful. Their CEO, Ryan Gellert, said that

> We are a for-profit enterprise, but we're committed to using our business to do more than just make money.[11]

Furthermore, Gellert believes that "unrestrained" capitalism is to blame for many of today's ills, from social inequalities to ecological disasters.[12] Gellert's words are not hyperbole. Patagonia once advertised "Don't buy this jacket" to encourage consumers to extend the life of their old clothes by fixing them. Counterintuitively the ad actually *increased* sales 30% and enhanced the company's reputation by encouraging responsible consumption.[13] A section in the company's website called "Buy Less, Demand More" educates customers about the practices they ought to seek from clothing manufacturers (including data that shows 10% of pollution causing the climate crisis is from the clothing industry).

Another section called "Worn Wear" sells used Patagonia clothing. Doing so extends a product's life by at least two years and reduces the water, waste, and carbon footprint by 73%.[14] Patagonia has succeeded with developing brand advocates not because they advertise to them (the company spends little on advertising) but because they have spent decades honing their engagement with their stakeholders (customers, outdoor groups, environmental causes...).

Patagonia has been ahead of the curve when it comes to environmental responsibility and is a role model for other businesses. The broader consumer market sees sustainability and responsibility as essential qualities they expect in businesses. A 2021 Edelman survey of 14,000 consumers in 14 countries found that 66% were "belief-driven" buyers that seek brands able to address global problems. 61% will advocate for brands they trust. Another Edelman report (2020) showed that 71% of respondents said trust would be lost if a company puts profits over people.

> *Those brands emphasizing only functional aspects earn an Edelman Brand Trust Score of 27 but those changing culture achieve a score of 65. Consumers are 4.5 times more likely to buy if a brand addresses human rights, 4x more likely if it speaks out on systemic racism and 3.5x more likely if it takes on economic inequality.*[15]

Your efforts to nurture stakeholders as advocates will pay dividends if they see your societal engagement as genuine. You are likely to *increase* your financial gain because people are seeking companies that demonstrate responsibility, which will attract more stakeholder advocates, inspiring a virtuous cycle of value creation. After graduate school I joined Nike's outdoor group (known as All Conditions Gear [ACG]), which had lackluster sales at the time because we had relied on tooling and designs borrowed mostly from other sports categories. The outdoor market perceived us as pretenders riding on the coattails of Nike's better-known sports categories. To fix this business, we engaged with outdoor athletes and retailers through a series of gatherings to learn their perspective and get their direct input. It was clear that unless we invested in products designed specifically for outdoor athletes (cycling, trail running, hiking, mountain biking, water sports...), we would remain pretenders in a market where credibility is critical. Over many months of prototyping, we developed products that the skeptical outdoor audience began to see as credible. Ultimately, the efforts paid off and we vaulted to the top of the outdoor market, converting skeptics to advocates. It would not have happened had we not made the genuine effort to understand outdoor market stake-holders, treat them as trusted advisors, and then revamp our product line.

## MEANING

*Meaning* describes the ability to understand, empathize, and connect compassionately with customers, then introducing solutions that grasp the need in the moment to create a following. Finding meaning in our work is crucial to our long-term health since much of our individual identities are wrapped up in our careers. When work becomes routine, we tend to lose interest and seek new challenges. Deloitte research (2019) found that 87% of employees seek meaning in their work.[16] If the work we're doing is impactful and we believe in the company's aspiration, then we gain greater meaning that also fuels our discretionary effort. People's definitions of what comprises meaning does differ, but stimulating alignment between an employee and their work is crucial. The stronger the alignment, the more likely the employee will feel that their work has meaning.

In the twentieth century if a businessperson asked you "what gives you meaning?" you would have walked quickly away. Business, as the thinking went, *means business* (always said emphatically). A search for meaning was considered utopian, and certainly not something the serious business professional sought. The twenty-first century is far different. Meaning is strengthened when people see a clear connection between what they highly value and what they choose to spend time doing. As you deepen your stakeholder engagement, you'll need to understand what they value, what gives their lives meaning, and what they define as impactful contribution. Chapter 6 described contribution at work from an employee perspective. The focus here is primarily on non-employee stakeholders.

Business schools teach that managers must *position* their businesses to the market. Positioning was a technique to strengthen awareness in the market about your company's identity. Most of us don't think about companies every waking moment so positioning messages helped communicate your company's most memorable characteristics. That was much easier in the pre-social media era when "company-out" messages were the communications standard, but far harder today when the power to confirm or deny reputations rests with stake-holders, not the company. This poses a challenge for fixed mindset business leaders who remain anchored to traditional marketing thinking because slick corporate promotion is seen today as bullshit, and not engaging.[17] Your company's reputation for credible ESG engagement is validated only when it is experienced by stakeholders who then advocate your virtues to others.

Cause, Advocacy, and Meaning is a more useful framework because it helps you identify what matters to your stakeholders so you can relate to them more thoughtfully and is crucial today since misunderstandings can lead to irreparable damage to your company's reputation if they don't perceive your efforts as genuine. Ask the following questions in your stakeholder/CAM research plan:

1. What do we need to understand about the plausible societal impacts from today's converging crises on our stakeholder community?

2. What ways can we engage meaningfully with stakeholders to learn about their concerns and interests?

3. Learn what stakeholders expect by asking 'how can we galvanize them to help us make the needed changes in our company?'

## Tools for Understanding Stakeholder Experiences

Empathy and touchpoints maps are invaluable visual tools for understanding and then engaging with stakeholders better.

### Empathy Map[18]

This is helpful in uncovering the underlying drivers of a given stakeholder's needs and avoiding sloppy generalizations and false assumptions. Several methods are used to understand stakeholder empathy. Typically, empathy maps place the subject stakeholder at the center of a flip chart and ask you to answer:

- What they are *seeing*

- What they are *thinking*

- What they are *saying*

- What they are *feeling*

- What they are *doing*

- What are their *pains*

- What are their *gains*

Using sticky notes affixed to the chart, once completed the empathy map is a colorful and memorable tool for visualizing your stakeholder's needs. Once you have created this, you'll be better able to identify how to translate your empathetic understanding into compassionate actions that address the stakeholder's needs.

### Company Touchpoints Map[19]

Touchpoints are the many tangible and intangible points of engagement stakeholders have with your company. Brainstorming sessions often identify hundreds of touchpoints. The volume of identified touchpoints reveals the many junctures between your company and your stakeholders that affect your reputation. The maps can become quite complex, with common connections and intersections among touchpoints that help you see their interdependencies, identifying weaker areas needing correction.

### Stakeholder Journey Map[20]

Each stakeholder experiences your company differently. A journey map shows the sequence of interactions throughout a given stakeholder's relationship with you, from pre-sale to purchase to implementation to post-sale follow up, and where things can go sideways if not nurtured.

### Systems Map[21]

This shows the solution development process and where ecosystem partners and internal experts add value, and where potential bottlenecks exist.

When you review each of these maps you'll see how they relate to each other, why understanding stakeholders helps identify touchpoints, where those touchpoints affect the stakeholder's journey, which can then help you adjust and refine your solution development process.

### So What?

We know that our effectiveness at nurturing a community of supportive stakeholders depends on our ability to engage with them. Meaningful and useful stakeholder engagement is the by-product of a well-planned, deliberate set of actions designed to strengthen our understanding of who they are and what factors are influencing their needs, anxieties, and aspirations. Khun Roongrote knows SCG's stakeholder community well, consequently he chose engaging with people as the first priority because addressing their wellbeing due to the Covid-19 crisis was the right thing to do. Patagonia understands that its stakeholders want companies to demonstrate a more responsible approach to using products in a world of finite resources. Each organization focused on asking different questions about their stakeholders, and the CAM framework provides the tools needed to visualize the impact of your stakeholder understanding on the force for good choices you will make. Let's build on your business's transformation in Chapter 11 by looking at ways to develop enriching environments both inside and outside the company.

## NOTES

1. Herbjørnsrud, D. (2016). First women of philosophy. *Aeon*, p. 5. Retrieved from https://aeon.co/essays/before-the-canon-the-non-european-women-who-founded-philosophy.
2. Based on 2021 author Interviews with Roongrote Rangsiyopash.
3. Davis, J. (2020). Marketing for the next normal. *DialogueReview*. Retrieved from https://dialoguereview.com/marketing-for-the-next-normal/.
4. Multiple sources. (1) Finkelstein, S. (2019). Don't be blinded by your own expertise. *Harvard Business Review*, pp. 3–4. Retrieved from https://www.hbsp.harvard.edu/product/R1903L-PDF-ENG?Ntt=don%27t%20be%20blinded%20by%20your%20own%20expertise. (2) Fjeld, J. (2017). How to test your assumptions. *MIT Sloan Management Review*. Retrieved from https://sloanreview.mit.edu/article/how-to-test-your-assumptions/.
5. Multiple sources: (1). Solly, M. (2020). 158 resources to understand racism in America. *Smithsonian Magazine*. Retrieved from https://www.smithsonianmag.com/history/158-resources-understanding-systemic-racism-america-180975029/. (2) Thomas, S. B., & Casper, E. (2019). *American Journal of Public Health*. Retrieved from https://www.ncbi.nlm.nih.gov/pmc/articles/PMC6727285/. (3) Worland, J. (2020). America's long overdue awakening to systemic racism. *Time Magazine*. Retrieved from https://time.com/5851855/systemic-racism-america/.
6. Altman, A. (2020). Why the killing of George Floyd sparked an American uprising. *Time Magazine*. Retrieved from https://time.com/5847967/george-floyd-protests-trump/.

7. Multiple sources: (1) Domonoske, C. (2016). Interactive redlining map zooms in on America history of discriminatin. NPR. Retrieved from https://www.npr.org/sections/thetwo-way/2016/10/19/498536077/interactive-redlining-map-zooms-in-on-americas-history-of-discrimination. (2) Gross, T. (2017). A 'forgotten history' of how the U.S. Government Segregated America. NPR. Retrieved from https://www.npr.org/2017/05/03/526655831/a-forgotten-history-of-how-the-u-s-government-segregated-america. (3) Anyaso, H. H. (2020). Racial discrimination in mortgage market persistent over last four decades. Northwestern University. Retrieved from https://news.northwestern.edu/stories/2020/01/racial-discrimination-in-mortgage-market-persistent-over-last-four-decades/.

8. Multiple sources: (1) Birkeland, B. Newsmax issues retraction and apology to dominion employee over election stories. NPR. Retrieved from https://www.npr.org/2021/04/30/992534968/newsmax-issues-retraction-and-apology-to-dominion-employee-over-election-stories. (2) Grimmer, J. (2021). No evidence for voter fraud: A guide to statistical claims about the 2020 election. Hoover Institution. Retrieved from https://www.hoover.org/research/no-evidence-voter-fraud-guide-statistical-claims-about-2020-election (for a deeper review, read the full analysis here: https://www.dropbox.com/s/o120sormtbw9w10/fraud_extended_public.pdf?dl=0). (3) Cohen, D. (2021). Former attorney general describes break with Trump on election fraud. Politico. Retrieved from https://www.politico.com/news/2021/06/27/barr-atlantic-trump-election-496513.

9. Alas, H. (2021). Report: Republican-led state legislatures pass dozens of restrictive voting laws in 2021. U.S. News & World Report. Retrieved from https://www.usnews.com/news/best-states/articles/2021-07-02/17-states-have-passed-restrictive-voting-laws-this-year-report-says.

10. Christensen, C. M., Hall, T., Dillon, K., & Duncan, D. (2016). Know your customers' "jobs to be done." Harvard Business Review. Retrieved from https://www.hbsp.harvard.edu/product/R1609D-PDF-ENG.

11. Balch, O. (2021). Patagonia CEO on leading a company with a cause. Raconteur. Retrieved from https://www.raconteur.net/corporate-social-responsibility/patagonia-ceo-on-leading-a-company-with-a-cause/.

12. See footnote 11.

13. Morin, C. (2020). Patagonia's customer base and the rise of an environmental ethos. CRM.org. Retrieved from https://crm.org/articles/patagonias-customer-base-and-the-rise-of-an-environmental-ethos.

14. No author. (2021). Patagonia website. Worn Wear. Retrieved from https://wornwear.patagonia.com/.

15. Edelman, R. (2021). Trust, the new brand equity. Retrieved from https://www.edelman.com/trust/2021-brand-trust/brand-equity.

16. Chevallier, E. (2020). Everyone wants meaning in their work-but how do you define it? The Conversations. Retrieved from https://theconversation.com/everyone-wants-meaning-in-their-work-but-how-do-you-define-it-128198.

17. Hsu, T. (2019). The advertising industry has a problem: People hate ads. The New York Times. Retrieved from https://www.nytimes.com/2019/10/28/business/media/advertising-industry-research.html.

18. Multiple sources: (1) No Date. Understand users through empathy maps. IBM Garage Methodology. Retrieved from https://www.ibm.com/garage/method/practices/think/practice_empathy_maps/. (2) No Date. Empathy planner. Stanford d.school. Retrieved from https://dschool.stanford.edu/resources/empathy-planner. (3) Bland, D. J. (2020). What is an empathy map? Accenture. Retrieved from https://www.accenture.com/us-en/blogs/software-engineering-blog/what-is-an-empathy-map.
19. No author. (2020). Customer touchpoints-the point of interaction between brands, businesses, products and customers. Interactive Design Foundation. Retrieved from https://www.interaction-design.org/literature/article/customer-touchpoints-the-point-of-interaction-between-brands-businesses-products-and-customers.
20. Amar, J., Raabe, J., & Roggenhofer, S. (2019). How to capture what the customer wants. McKinsey. Retrieved from https://www.mckinsey.com/business-functions/operations/our-insights/how-to-capture-what-the-customer-wants.
21. Dreier, L., Nabarro, D., & Nelson, J. (2019). Systems leadership for sustainable development: Strategies for achieving systemic change. Harvard Kennedy School Corporate Responsibility Initiative. pp. 15, 20. Retrieved from https://www.hks.harvard.edu/sites/default/files/centers/mrcbg/files/Systems%20Leadership.pdf.

# 11

# ENRICHING ENVIRONMENTS

*To see what light we receive from Nature to direct our Actions, and how far we are Naturally able to obey that Light.*[1]
—*Damaris Cudworth Masham*

Jonathan will never forget that first $150 he earned. He had always been fascinated by technology, read popular computing magazines, and he learned to program. His older brother was into technology, too, and Jonathan learned more by watching and working with him. Jonathan had an insatiable curiosity and by age 11 he had enough technology and programming know-how to write an electronic learning game based on the popular Speak & Spell device. It sold well, which is how he earned the $150, an enormous sum for a kid growing up in Dublin, Ireland. His dad, too, reinforced his passion for technology and creative innovation. As a teen his interests broadened further. His circle of friends changed and, like many teens, he got into music, learning guitar and piano. He formed a band and performed in local venues. Inwardly, Jonathan enjoyed the personal excitement from learning and writing new songs and, outwardly, he loved the atmosphere and buzz of playing to live audiences. More interesting opportunities arose. He was offered a university scholarship to study in the US. He and his brother started a pre-internet tech company. A few years later Jonathan applied for and received a US visa and his green card. Not long after that he was offered a technologist job with Coopers & Lybrand, which ultimately became PwC (PricewaterhouseCoopers), where he worked for many years. Jonathan embraced the rapid shifts and advances in technology at that time. PwC benefits helped pay for education, so he earned his PhD in Information Systems. He absolutely loved the opportunities his work in the company's technology innovation group provided, enabling him to work with inspiring colleagues on fascinating client projects. After PwC Jonathan joined O'Reilly Media and was then subsequently recruited to be Chief Information Officer for the City of Palo Alto, California. Government work would be different, and he wondered if it would be as vibrant as the private sector. But like everything else he had done Jonathan decided to jump at the opportunity, seeing it as a chance to learn about government work in a city considered the epicenter of high tech. Thinking he would stay for 3 years, he ended up staying for 7 years. Early in his tenure he was invited to speak at a conference in France and over time he found himself doing more speaking and audience workshops. As CIO for a city he was introduced to a wide range of smart cities issues, and his expertise grew. Media coverage and speaking engagements followed. He was recognized as one of the world's Top 100 CIOs. "Without question this government CIO job changed me," said Jonathan. Opportunities opened up with LinkedIn Learning, as did advising work with cities around the world, and he now works with a wide range of organizations, speaking at events and authoring best-selling books. Jonathan is fueled by his love of innovation and education, the by-product of a lifetime of enriching, supportive environments and his own, personal appetite for learning. From developing a Speak & Spell-Like software application to helping teach the world about the merits of smart cities Jonathan found his future.

What characterizes a smart city? Jonathan defines a smart city as "an urban community that uses new ideas and technology to create a better quality of life for everyone."[2] Singapore is a leading example. The city-state's aim is to be a smart nation. Sensors are throughout its commercial and residential infrastructures. Data are collected constantly, monitoring a wide range of activities, helping to improve energy usage, traffic flows, and overall quality of life. My family and I lived there for 15 years and loved it. As those who have lived there know, "everything works" in Singapore. Technology-related problems are rare. The country's smart city investments make it easier for people to enjoy work and life without the distractions from unreliable infrastructure. Singapore is not alone. Jonathan's work around the world helps leaders understand how to direct their urban investments toward improving well-being and quality of life.

## INTERNAL ENVIRONMENT

Borrowing from the spirit of *smart*, the following criteria summarize business practices I have seen work effectively for companies as they embark on new initiatives; in this case we'll apply it to helping improve your company's internal and external environmental footprints.

## S = Specific

Start by identifying specific areas in your operations where you can have the highest sustainable impact with minimal short-term disruption to support your "force for good" improvements. Focus on:

Embedding specifics into people performance: Introduce community support hours for employees as part of their benefits. There will be an accounting cost, but there will also be improvement in how local communities perceive your organization. Stop the quickest non-sustainable practices immediately. For example, stop the use of providing bottled water in plastic containers and replace with filtered water, as Thailand's SCG did in 2018. Nike's 'Reusable Dishware Program' encourages employees to stop using disposable containers and utensils. The program helped reduce single-use containers by 16,000 pounds per quarter.[3] These are small moves initially, but they are powerful symbolically and practically. While these new practices are being implemented plan the staging and sequencing of your larger, more substantial operating changes.

## M = Material

Material refers to reasoning (material knowledge), not physical forms. Focus on the meaning and measure of your intended ESG impact, including embedding specific sustainable requirements into the design of your solutions. Your "force for good" criteria must be relevant to your company's aspiration and meaningful to your stakeholders. Determine how to help, or exit agreements, with partners lacking reliable sustainability practices.

## A = Advance

Businesses are designed to prosper from selling solutions customers want at a price that returns a reasonable profit, the proceeds of which are reinvested in the business. At least, that's the theory. But we know that doesn't always happen and has led to shareholder enrichment and share buyback-dominated actions that create short-term gains at the expense of long-term organizational health. To make advances you have to take risks. Since we're still human, we make mistakes. Punishing a failure is usually not a great development lesson. Before you pass judgment, you owe it to your employees to examine the context and related factors that may have impacted their performance.

## R = Resourceful

Recognize and capture lessons from people who demonstrate ingenuity such as imaginatively combining existing materials, stretching the budget, and eliminating unused resources (see Imagination Ambassador in Chapter 3). Have a macro-view of your ecosystem, with all partners aligned on using sustainable materials and production simplification. Kroger and Walgreens, two US-based grocery and pharmacy chains, work in partnership with waste management company TerraCycle to sell products to consumers in reusable containers that are used until emptied, then retrieved for reuse. While this service, called "Loop," is only available in a regional US geography and such initiatives need rapid scaling to achieve a meaningful material impact,[4] it serves as a useful test case for *smart*er partner business models. Intel buys conflict materials used in the production of their chips in countries like the Democratic Republic of the Congo (DRC). Rather than abandoning sourcing, which would have had significantly negative implications for employment with other legal mining operations and ecosystem partners, Intel instead created provisions in the U.S.'s Dodd–Frank Act that help track and disclose similar mineral sourcing throughout the entire industry. The result was a change in how the company, and sector competitors, determine their sourcing criteria, mining safety protocols, and labor practices.[5] Ricoh, the Japanese electronics giant, projects that by 2050 there will be a shortage of the raw materials they need for manufacturing, so the company is now reorganizing its business model around life cycle analysis, which assesses the environmental impact at each stage of a product's life cycle. Simultaneously, Ricoh is working with customers to help them rethink their energy usage, carbon footprint, and product refurbishment and recycling technologies. Their 2050 target is to reduce virgin resource use by nearly 90%.[6]

## T = Teachable

Pay forward by sharing lessons learned from your sustainable efforts to build a healthy, self-perpetuating community of concerned stakeholders. Each new generation of employees should be able to easily learn from the prior generation and be ready to teach the next. Turning data into memorable stories helps. We can see data in a bar chart, but it takes true storytelling to explain what the data reveal. In 1997 after returning as Apple's CEO Steve Jobs reduced 350 products to fewer than 10, eliminated business unit general manager roles and silos, thereby enabling people to collaborate more effectively. At the time the company had $7 billion in revenue. In 2021 Apple's revenues were $365 billion and, at the time of this writing, their market capitalization had grown to more than $2.9 trillion.[7] The story Steve told developers and employees in 1997 helped to laser-focus the company's innovation strategy. He compared Apple at the time to a farm with animals running in different directions, but with no destination.[8] He said that focus is about saying "no," not "yes." Years later Jobs said "I'm actually as proud of the things we haven't done as the things I have done. Innovation is saying no to 1,000 things. You have to pick carefully."[9]

Picking carefully includes making the workplace safer, especially with the lessons learned from Covid-19. Given today's pandemic, healthier workplaces with improved ventilation, reconfigured open spaces, and more astute policies to ensure safer and more hygienic office environments are emerging. A Harvard survey (2019) found that wellness programs in the US had limited success because companies often focused on the wrong perks. Employees wanted improved workplace basics: better air quality, natural light, and the ability to personalize their work areas as it turns out these factors can reduce absenteeism by 4 days per year.[10] Since that survey the pandemic has changed behavior further. Masking, regular handwashing, and vaccines help reduce the chances of disease contagion spreading, thereby better protecting employees and visitors. Becoming more sustainable and more socially responsible doesn't seem like an option…it is a vital necessity.

With Covid-19 variants it is understandable that companies are wondering how to ensure their offices are safer for work than they were prepandemic. The pandemic has forced many people to work remotely, and it is likely that a full return to the workplace as it used to be is unlikely. Even before Covid-19 company facility designs worldwide were witnessing a revolution, with environmentally savvy features, clever use of interior spaces, a host of earth-friendlier materials, and architectural approaches that provide unique and healthier environments. These advances remain important, but eliminating all risks in the workplace is not possible or realistic. The U.S. Centers for Disease Control and Prevention (CDC) has two helpful strategies to help companies think through their return to business approach, summarized below: Prevention through Design (PtD) and Hierarchy of Controls.

PtD aims to prevent or greatly reduce harm to employees at work by including potential risks at work into the design of facilities and workspaces within. If you are planning to build new offices or remodel existing ones, then the intent of PtD is to have you first identify any potential risks and design them out of the planning or minimize them significantly.[11] The Hierarchy of Controls are methods of escalation from least effective to most effective for reducing injury or illness risk factors in the workplace, ranging from PPE (least effective) to elimination of hazards (most effective).[12] PtD and Hierarchy of Controls give your company a starting point for making a healthier workplace. Are these expensive? The answer is "it depends." Your primary concern must be the health and well-being of your employees and anybody who visits your facilities. The additional costs pale in comparison to the physical injury or even death that poor designs might cause.

Of course, a healthy company culture encompasses several critical qualities beyond just prevention and control hierarchies. Work with employees to integrate *aspiration* through design, *preparation* through design, and being *proactive* through design as important new culture practices for your company. For example, identify those current practices that are contrary to your aspiration and design them out of your organization. Prepare policies that describe how you will treat all people as part of being your force for good aspiration. Proactively invite employees to offer ways to improve shortcomings in the workplace. Diversity, equity, and inclusion (DEI) are essential to a healthy workplace and a well-functioning society. Policies that provide people with access to opportunities irrespective of gender, race, religion, disability, or sexual identity, and ensure equal pay for equal work are obvious, needed and still missing from so many companies. You'll need to overcome entrenched biases that can undermine what are basic human rights in today's modern workplace.

Your company's success can no longer be measured just in profits and shareholder returns because those measures are dependent on healthy employees. As the world struggles through multiple crises there are exemplar organizations doing the right thing. Research by *MIT Sloan Management Review* and Glassdoor (2015–2020) of Culture 500[13] companies found that the quality of communication from senior management was viewed positively by employees and increased significantly in the first quarter of the pandemic in 2020. 88% of employees said leaders were honest and transparent in the first six months of Covid-19, compared to only 46% at the same time frame the prior year.[14] Employees were 57% likelier to speak favorably about the company's ethical behavior, with 51% more likely to discuss their company's regulatory compliance.[15] Seeing companies respond to a clear existential threat with an employee-first mindset suggests that companies are indeed capable of doing the right thing, quickly, and decisively.

## EXTERNAL ENVIRONMENT

Your external environment is demonstrated by how your company shows up in the world through its operations, facilities, distribution, ecosystem part-nerships, virtual environments, and force for good disclosures, as guided by your aspiration.

When visitors enter Vancouver, Canada's Convention Centre, they are entering the world's first double Platinum LEED certified convention facility. This is a unique designation that means a building met the earlier LEED Platinum and more recent (and more rigorous) LEED v4 Platinum certifica-tions. To achieve LEED v4 they improved waste management, reduced water usage and energy efficiency, achieving a 30% increase in its blackwater (waste) treatment and 75% waste diversion (vs. 50% the prior year). More than 900 light fixtures were changed to LEDs. These efforts reduced the amount of potable water used by 38% (the equivalent of approximately 300,000 toilet flushes) and reduced energy usage from the more efficient fixtures in the facilities.[16]

Boston Consulting Group research (2020) found that during the first few months of Covid-19 87% of consumers wanted companies to demonstrate improved integration of environmental needs across all operations[17] and 51% of investors wanted companies to support ESG even at the risk of reduced earnings per share.[18] PwC (2021) found that 83% of consumers want ESG as a best practice in companies, 91% of business leaders want their business to lead by example by supporting ESG initiatives and, similar to other studies I cited earlier, 86% of employees want to work for companies that share the same concerns about major issues as they have.[19] The European Union was the first region to enact new regulations on sustainable investing in 2021 called the Sustainable Finance Disclosure Regulation (SFDR), requiring fund managers to report details on the investment criteria with the intent to prevent greenwashing.[20] Soon thereafter, the US Securities and Exchange Commission (SEC), led by its Chairman Gary Gensler, pushed for mandatory climate disclosures for all public companies. Specific climate metrics were still being defined, but despite expected pushback from industry and conservative lawmakers more detailed disclosures appear headed for approval.[21] The European Commission (EC) updated their 2030 climate and energy framework, with more aggressive targets for reducing greenhouse gas emissions, increasing renewable energy, and improving energy efficiency.[22] But even with the US's SEC and the EC working through various mechanisms to support greater accountability, the difficulty of getting businesses to change cannot be overstated. The data provide you with the intellectual cover validating why your company is trying to change, and that's important. But it is also abstract. You and I can read that data and understand why this matters. Translating that into how your business becomes part of the solution means improving how stakeholders are experiencing your company, including what it is like engaging with your products and services, your marketing, your physical spaces, your value chain partners, and your employees. Moving from abstraction to impactful, meaningful experience is as detail-oriented as any other day-to-day logistics your company has run for years, except that you are redirecting those efforts toward ESG-inspired initiatives.

## PERCEPTIONS

Remember that perception is reality. The environments you create will help shape how people view you. And it helps that ESG-driven companies have better growth and valuations by 10–20%.[23]

## Employees

Great Place to Work® ranks company workplaces, which serves as an indicator of employee happiness. ESG makes employees happier and improves shareholder returns. London Business School (2012) found that over 25 years companies in the top 100 returned 2.3%–3.8% higher annual returns than competitors.[24] The Great Place to Work® criteria are a helpful guide for your company. As an employee at REI said, "There are a few places that come close to the level of passion that I've experienced at REI; a passion for the outdoors, excellence, doing the right thing, and for purpose over profit."[25] Imagine a similar sentiment from your employees.

## Customers

88% of consumers want companies to help them improve their environmental and social contribution,[26] and every company touchpoint influences what customers experience. The evidence shows that people expect your company to be a positive societal actor, so make sure all touchpoints are aligned, not disconnected, whether it is in your direct control or that of partners.

## Shareholders

85% of investors include ESG in their criteria.[27] Shareholders care that you make money, and how you make it. Shareholder forums are influential environments where they can experience your leaders as a group of professionals they are entrusting to increase your business's value and, thereby, evaluate your company's ongoing investment potential. More companies and shareholders are aligning around societal value. As Adam Grealish, Betterment's Director of Investing, says (2020) "The collective action starts to become powerful. If I'm an investor, I may not be tilting the scales on my own, but at the collective level it starts to matter."[28]

## Value Chain Partners

Nearly 70% of your ESG impact is due to your partners.[29] The environment you and your partners create reflects on your company, affects how trust is engendered across the ecosystem, and accrues financial benefits. Puma, the sports company, launched a sustainable finance program in 2016 that rewards suppliers for their sustainability efforts.[30] As BSR's (Business for Social Responsibility) Charlotte Bancilhon said about PUMA, "...during the first year of its sustainable supply chain finance program, it provided more than $100m in lower financing costs to 15% of its suppliers – those that achieved a high sustainability score. The impact for sustainability can't be overlooked: By PUMA's internal accounting, 94% of its environmental impact is in its supply chain."[31] Through this program PUMA is accelerating their suppliers' transformation to more sustainable practices.

## So What?

The societal value motive is not a solo undertaking. It demands that business leaders step into the chasm between destructive and constructive practices by influencing not just their boards and employees to change, but all stakeholders in their ecosystem. Just as company leaders preach internally for their employees to celebrate diverse perspectives, they must role-model this very same behavior to bring their partners and stakeholders across their entire business environment along.

Bombarding customer senses with choice has led to mass consumerism and a disposable mentality, creating waste and rampant materialism. Companies must align internal environments (facilities, distribution, cultural benefits ...) with external (outlets, stakeholder atmospherics, smart packaging, and more) to build trust with stakeholders. We are in control of the choices we make about how we define our company's role in improving society. And those choices will affect the quality of the workplace and external environments where we work and live, with society deciding whether our efforts are successful.

Questions that will help you evaluate your company's operating environments:

1. How do people inside see and experience us and what must we do to transform these areas to ensure we are practicing what we preach?

2. How do people outside see and experience us and what must we do to transform these areas to ensure we are delivering not just what we promise, but also what creates positive, enduring value for society?

In Chapter 12 you'll gain insight about how your company's transformation will affect the solutions you develop to generate positive value for society.

## NOTES

1. Warren, K. (2009). An unconventional history of western philosophy: Conversations between men and women philosophers. p. 234. Retrieved from https://books.google.com/books?id=RUBTOI2OWSUC&dq=To+see+what+light+we+receive+from+Nature+to+direct+our+Actions,+and+how+far+we+are+Naturally+able+to+obey+that+Light&source=gbs_navlinks_s.
2. Based on 2021 author Interviews with Jonathan Reichental.
3. No author. (2020). 6 examples of sustainability in the workplace (and their impact). Recycle Coach. Retrieved from https://recyclecoach.com/blog/6-examples-of-sustainability-in-the-workplace-and-their-impact/.
4. Frazee, G. (2019). 4 reasons it's hard to become a sustainable business. PBS. Retrieved from https://www.pbs.org/newshour/economy/making-sense/4-reasons-its-hard-to-become-a-sustainable-business.
5. Shotts, K., & Melvin, S. (2015). Looking inside: Intel and conflict materials. Stanford Graduate School of Business. Retrieved from https://www.gsb.stanford.edu/faculty-research/case-studies/looking-inside-intel-conflict-minerals.
6. Hoffman, A. J. (2018). The next phase of business sustainability. *Stanford Social Innovation Review*. Retrieved from https://ssir.org/articles/entry/the_next_phase_of_business_sustainability.
7. Yahoo! Finance. (2021). Retrieved from https://finance.yahoo.com/quote/AAPL/financials?p=AAPL.
8. Shah, D. (2021). 16 brilliant insights from Steve Jobs Keynote Circa 1997. Retrieved from https://www.onstartups.com/tabid/3339/bid/58082/16-Brilliant-Insights-From-Steve-Jobs-Keynote-Circa-1997.aspx.
9. Mejia, Z. (2018). Steve Jobs: Here's what most people get wrong about focus. CNBC. Retrieved from https://www.cnbc.com/2018/10/02/steve-jobs-heres-what-most-people-get-wrong-about-focus.html.
10. Meister, J. C. (2019). Survey: What employees want most from their workspaces. *Harvard Business Review*. Retrieved from https://hbr.org/2019/08/survey-what-employees-want-most-from-their-workspaces.
11. No author. (2013). National institute for occupational safety & health. prevention and design. Retrieved from https://www.cdc.gov/niosh/topics/ptd/.
12. No author. (2015). Hierarchy of controls. Centers for Disease Control & Prevention. Retrieved from https://www.cdc.gov/niosh/topics/hierarchy/default.html.

13. The Culture 500 are companies with top-performing cultures based on 1.2 million Glassdoor reviews using MIT's Natural Language Processing (NLP) methodology. These companies employ a total of 34 million people. For more information, visit: https://sloanreview.mit.edu/projects/measuring-culture-in-leading-companies/.

14. Sull, D., & Sull, C. (2020). How companies are winning on culture during COVID-19. *MIT Sloan Management Review*. Retrieved from https://sloanreview.mit.edu/article/how-companies-are-winning-on-culture-during-covid-19/.

15. See footnote 14.

16. No author. (2017). Pushing boundaries in sustainability: World's first double LEED platinum convention center. Retrieved from https://www.vancouverconventioncentre.com/news/pushing-boundaries-in-sustainability-worlds-first.

17. Kachaner, N., Nielsen, J., Portafaix, A., & Rodzko, F. (2020). The pandemic is heightening environmental awareness. Boston Consulting Group. Retrieved from https://www.bcg.com/publications/2020/pandemic-is-heightening-environmental-awareness.

18. Unnikrishnan, S., Bigs, C., & Singh, N. (2020). Sustainability matters now more than ever for consumer companies. Boston Consulting Group. Retrieved from https://www.bcg.com/publications/2020/sustainability-matters-now-more-than-ever-for-consumer-companies.

19. No author. (2021). PwC. Beyond compliance: Consumers and employees want business to do more on ESG. Retrieved from https://www.pwc.com/us/en/services/consulting/library/consumer-intelligence-series/consumer-and-employee-esg-expectations.html.

20. Norton, L. P. (2021). New EU regulations on sustainable investing could hit U.S. Funds Soon. Barron's. Retrieved from https://www.barrons.com/articles/eu-regulations-sustainable-investing-us-mutual-funds-51615567546.

21. Michaels, D. (2021). SEC wants more climate disclosures. Businesses are preparing for a fight. *The Wall Street Journal*. Retrieved from https://www.wsj.com/articles/climate-fight-brews-as-sec-moves-toward-mandate-for-risk-disclosure-11624267803.

22. European Commission. (2021). 2030 climate & energy framework. Retrieved from https://ec.europa.eu/clima/policies/strategies/2030_en.

23. Cherel-Bonnenmaison, C., Erlandsson, G., Ibach, B., & Spiller, P. (2021). Buying into a more sustainable value chain. McKinsey. Retrieved from https://www.mckinsey.com/business-functions/operations/our-insights/buying-into-a-more-sustainable-value-chain.

24. Edmans, A. (2012). The link between job satisfaction and firm value, with implications for corporate social responsibility. *Academy of Management Perspectives*, 26(4), 1–9, journals.aom.org.

25. No author. (2020). Fortune 100 best companies to Work For® 2020. Retrieved from https://www.greatplacetowork.com/best-workplaces/100-best/2020.

26. Townsend, S. (2018). 88% of consumers want you to help them make a difference. Forbes. Retrieved from https://www.forbes.com/sites/solitaireto

wnsend/2018/11/21/consumers-want-you-to-help-them-make-a-difference/?
sh=def953f69547.
27. Venkataramani, S. (2021). The ESG imperative: 7 factors for finance leaders
to consider. Gartner. Retrieved from https://www.gartner.com/smarterwi
thgartner/the-esg-imperative-7-factors-for-finance-leaders-to-consider.
28. Adamczyk, A. (2020). BlackRock CEO says sustainability is the 'top issue'
for investors-here's what that means for your money. CNBC Make It.
Retrieved from https://www.cnbc.com/2020/01/14/blackrocks-larry-fink-says-
sustainability-is-the-top-investor-issue.html.
29. Cherel-Bonnenmaison, C., Erlandsson, G., Ibach, B., & Spiller, P. (2021).
Buying into a more sustainable value chain. McKinsey. Retrieved from https://
www.mckinsey.com/business-functions/operations/our-insights/buying-into-a-
more-sustainable-value-chain.
30. No author. (2016). PUMA launches financing program to reward suppliers
for sustainability performance. SustainableBrands. Retrieved from https://
sustainablebrands.com/read/organizational-change/puma-launches-financing
-program-to-reward-suppliers-for-sustainability-performance.
31. Volkman, S. (no date). Sustainable supply chain finance: Q&A with Charlotte Bancilhon, Manager, BSR. The SustainAbility Institute by ERM.
Retrieved from https://www.sustainability.com/thinking/sustainable-supply-
chain-finance-qa-with-charlotte-bancilhon-manager-bsr/.

# 12

# DELIVERING SOLUTIONS

*Great difficulties may be surmounted by patience and perseverance.*[1]
*—Abigail Adams*

*"We need to be fully conscious of the full life cycle of the products on the planet, not just the tail pipe exhaust part"* says Kevin Czinger, Founder of Divergent 3D, a Los Angeles-based 3D manufacturer, summarizing his whole-systems view philosophy. Divergent 3D manufactures cars, currently. Kevin is taking the climate crisis head-on, doing much more than producing EVs (electric vehicles). What was his call to action? To this day, vehicles are built using the same logic and sequential methods as Henry Ford first used over 100 years ago. Factories with massive carbon footprints taking up acres of land and producing huge amounts of harmful carbon emissions still dominate. Even with the excitement around the advent of EVs the core manufacturing process is derived from practices developed in the early 1900s. Kevin and his team examined every phase and each assumption in the production system, including supplier inputs at each stage, to innovate an entirely new approach within a closed-loop cycle, essentially blowing apart the auto industry's century-old business model. Divergent 3D uses new technologies to dramatically decrease material and energy usage and, consequently, has literally reinvented every life-cycle stage of vehicle manufacturing. Kevin believes we must be open to all technologies to help manufacturing overall, not just EVs. The result is a production method called Divergent Adaptive Production System (DAPS™), a radically new, more sustainable approach to manufacturing that is protected by over 475 patents filings.

Divergent 3D's name was inspired by Charles Darwin's divergent evolution, the process by which dissimilar traits evolve from a common ancestry to adapt to contextual pressures. The common ancestry is vehicle manufacturing. The contextual pressures include the climate crisis, global warming, high carbon emissions, and pollution. The solution is diverging from traditional auto manufacturing techniques. For more than 100 years we have assumed that the way to make cars, or machinery, or any other large-scale production of widgets, required enormous factories with extensive and expensive assembly lines. Turns out that's not the case. The complexity of the challenge Kevin undertook cannot be overstated. How do you unwind decades of industrial practices and replace them with entirely new systems and routines? Divergent 3D has raised over $150 million and is not just building cars with significantly lower emissions but reinventing the automobile manufacturing process by using new technologies to substantially reduce the material and energy required at each stage of vehicle production. DAPS™ results in a greener car that is up to 90% lighter than equivalent cars, and safer (stronger materials in the production process plus the lighter weight reduces wear and tear) and from an operating standpoint lowers your capital risk, shortens your product cycle, and replaces parts at a lower cost.

Kevin is the youngest of five siblings from a working-class Ohio family. His parents were World War II veterans. He was extremely shy growing up, and perpetually curious. In secondary school he learned about environmental stewardship, learning an early age that humans have a responsibility, given the impact of the built world on the environment, for maintaining the diversity of life. He recalled being influenced from watching the BBC series 'The Ascent of Man', imbuing him with a sense of the promise of human ingenuity. Kevin is a fascinating person to talk to whose enthusiasm for reinventing an entire industry and manufacturing model is infectious. His older brothers were car fans, so he grew up working on all kinds of vehicles, plus racing them competitively. He developed into a successful athlete, playing football at Yale where he was MVP in the Ivy league. His spent his early career as lawyer trying securities fraud cases, then moved into investment banking, venture capital, and private equity. Throughout he has been animated by a larger societal value motive. In 2006 he cofounded a battery design and EV manufacturing company, set up as a JV in China, giving him a chance to think deeply about the design and manufacture of vehicles in a very hands-on way. It was clear that technology, company location, distribution, how people are employed, environmental impact, the means of production, and more are structured around a twentieth-century business model. The structure of those factories meant that any change was very expensive because tooling changed, designs changed, materials changed, so you had to lock yourself into a design for 7–8 years and build enormous volumes to make the changes financially viable. He wondered how to disrupt this pattern, including how to cut every single cost. In short, he took a clean sheet of paper approach to imagine a better, modern system. Auto manufacturing is an analog system and is the most fundamentally broken industry. Hundreds of millions of dollars are spent stamping tools and custom fixturing to hold components together, built on a half-mile long assembly line. In form and function, it is the exact opposite of digital. Kevin studied total system economics to develop his own architecture for a universal constructor. Some technologies were years away from practicality, so he had to think through creative ways to collapse that development cycle. Fast forward to today and DAPS™ produces structures that are 20–70% lighter mass and higher performing. It is a fully digitalized manufacturing system using AI that develops auto structures using purpose-built materials (put only where they're needed) then assembles them with ZERO switchover time from one structure to the next. DAPS™ does not waste an atom of energy, literally. Materials can be reatomized and turned back into a critical component. DAPS™ is the first foundational manufacturing structure for a circular economy with closed-loop material flows. The initial proofs of concept are impressive: in August 2021 Divergent 3D's 21C hypercar set a production car lap record at Laguna Seca, faster than any other car. The 21C goes from 0 to 60 in less than 2 seconds, with a top speed of 253 mph. In short, Divergent 3D has proven it can build a high-quality, high-performance vehicle using DAPS™.

Longer-term Kevin envisions DAPS™ located in high-density cities around the world, linked to each other through a global datasphere, contextualized to local needs. As each DAPS™ node talks to the others they are perpetually learning, adapting, and improving, and ultimately upgrading themselves, creating a sustainable manufacturing system that is in harmony with the planet and evenly distributes technology, plus DAPS™ gives more people access to the means for producing things. That is no small vision, and the amazing part is that the 21C has proven the technology today. Kevin and Divergent 3D epitomize the kind of dedicated thinking and hard work needed to create a sustainable, impactful, and practical business model equal to the challenges we face in dealing with today's global crises.[2]

## SOLUTIONS

We'll focus here on the questions you must ask on your path to new solution development that helps your company make the permanent shift into a force for good. Maybe your interest is social injustice, like the Bridge Institute's Mac McKenzie. Or perhaps your cause is reducing your carbon footprint, like Divergent 3D's Kevin Czinger. Or maybe the Covid-19 pandemic has focused your attention on helping people by providing necessary, life-saving equipment and medicines, like SCG's Khun Roongrote. Success is not automatic simply because you want to do the right thing and you believe people everywhere will recognize your goodwill and consequently buy your solutions. It's not that easy. The era of "build it and they will buy it" company planning is obsolete. Today's marketplace is smart, and people within have access to a wealth of news and information about companies and their reputations. Too many firms have lost credibility because of business practices that wreak havoc and harm society. Today, stakeholders buy into (not just buy) the promise of better futures that the company represents *if* the company can show how its solutions answer specific questions.

2018 research from NYU's Stern Center for Sustainable Business found that 54.7% of the growth in consumer-packaged goods between 2015 and 2019 came from sustainably marketed products and grew "7.1 times faster compared to products not marketed as sustainable."[3] Since you still want your company to make money you'll be heartened to know that this research found that sustainable products have a nearly 40% price premium over nonsustainably marketed ones.[4] Momentum is growing. The market share of sustainably-marketed products grew from 13.7% in 2015 to 16.8% in 2020.[5] The 2019–2020 two-year CAGR for sustainably marketed products was 42% compared to 39% for nonsustainably marketed products.[6] Their findings concluded that consumers are voting with their dollars against brands that are unsustainable.

We marvel when an ingenious innovation arrives and lets us do something we didn't even realize we needed or wanted. Edwin Land's instant photography wasn't sought by customers, nor was Apple's iPhone that combined music with a phone and a computer, yet both captured our imagination, opening us up to new ways of socializing with other people and enjoying life on the go. They were solutions, but not to an evident problem. Today's crises are evident and innovative solutions are not. But that should not lead you to hopelessness and despair. Nor should it inspire false hope that another Steve Jobs will save the day. Part of the solution lies within each of us to change our routines and open our minds to new ways of thinking and behaving to have an impact. And that's a good start. Just as importantly we need institutions across societies to collaborate on enough experiments to see what works. This is where the opportunity lies for all businesses, and your company, because as the data show, people are asking for businesses to help. 61% of consumers say they appreciated it when companies spent money to keep them updated on how they helped others during the Covid-19 pandemic.[7] This is where your trusted stakeholder relationships will give you an edge. Select specific stakeholders whose influence and guidance stands out and who are willing to join you in test and learn experiments as you prototype solutions. Remember that if you've developed trust around common force-for-good interests, then those selected stakeholders will become built-in believers with a vested interest in seeing your solutions succeed.

But don't wait for the perfect solution or the perfect combination of stakeholders. No amount of criteria or data will give you 100% confidence and assurance that you've chosen correctly. You learn by taking initial steps and getting to know each other to see what works. We know the many vexing global challenges: solving the climate crisis; advocating for and addressing social injustice; eliminating economic inequality; creating accessible educational opportunities, and more. Your company's task is to translate stakeholder insights into solutions guided by your aspiration and the societal value you aim to create.

Skånetrafiken is a Swedish regional public transportation authority that aspired to reinvent the urban-travel experience from beginning to end on public buses and trains for people living in Region Skåne. Their aim is to be 100% climate neutral. Skånetrafiken is comprised of several government agencies and local transport companies collaborating in support of making regional travel sustainable. More than 465,000 trips are made every day and 170 million per year. They have incorporated numerous innovations for passengers, including phone chargers, cup holders, and even sensors passengers can use for signaling bus drivers about their next stop, without having to touch buttons. Buses run on renewable fuels or electricity, reducing their climate emissions by 90%, with 100% renewable fuels the short-term goal. Eco-friendly fabrics are in all city-based buses. Because of the proximity of bus stops to urban residential areas, studies have proven that people are not only reducing their use of personal transportation but also have increased their daily walks to and from stations. Interestingly, the use of the Skånetrafiken transportation system is breaking down societal barriers between ethnic groups since the buses and trains are plentiful and within walking distance, encouraging people to travel to different parts of the region. Skånetrafiken's promotions highlight the positive impact of choosing public transportation. For example, you would need 243 train trips to emit the same amount of greenhouse gases as a single car. Or 107 bus trips. One bus can transport 64 passengers, equivalent to approximately 49 cars. 10,300 people make the daily train trip between two towns, Malmö and Hässleholm, a journey that would have otherwise required over 7,900 cars and would have taken 38 km of street space.[8] Messages like these provide an invaluable education to the local public, encouraging their sustainable behavior.

In recent years, PepsiCo pivoted away from many of their traditional brands and toward sustainable new products. PepsiCo's Sustainable Farming and Regenerative Agriculture Programs bring farmers into its production ecosystem by providing them with training and resource support to implement state-of-the-art farming practices that secure soil health and enhance biodiversity, significantly reducing the harm caused by a century of farming practices that depleted soils of critical nutrients and caused environmental damage from deforestation.[9]

Procter & Gamble innovated new cold water detergents that reduce energy consumption and will eliminate 4.25 million metric tons of greenhouse gas emissions by 2030 that are currently pumped into the atmosphere from existing warm and hot water laundry uses.[10]

Ecolab, an 80-year-old firm selling cleaners, heard that clean water access was a growing concern from its customers. Rather than doubling down on selling more cleaners into new markets, the company bought Nalco, a water technology company. Soon, Ecolab was helping its customers use water more efficiently and responsibly. Ecolab's market capitalization grew from $12 billion in 2011 to $55 billion in 2018 as markets saw the positive impact of their solutions on reducing water demand, particularly in water-challenged geographies like the western US, southern India, and select countries in central to north Africa.[11]

Each of these companies are tackling hugely complex problems and have found new ways to reinvent product manufacturing and service delivery.

Why not join them? As a thought experiment, get together with your team and/or other people you trust and ask the following big-picture questions:

1. What can your company do to act as boldly as companies like Divergent 3D and Skånetrafiken?

2. What systemic changes must you make in how you conceive, design, produce, and deliver solutions?

3. Which people and partners can help you create new solutions?

If it helps, then reconfigure these questions to be more pertinent to your company but don't shy away from asking them just because they invite complex comments. Like Kevin Czinger, try clean-sheeting your business. What would you do completely differently if you could wave a magic wand? Then use the VALUES framework below to help guide more penetrating planning.

## Creating Solutions: The *VALUES* Framework

The VALUES framework are a set of principles to guide how your company develops solutions.

1. *Visualize:* Picture the problem and state your vision for addressing it. Doing so creates a visual frame of reference to help people imagine that better future.
   Norrsken envisions a world of entrepreneurs creating *impact unicorns,* businesses addressing one of the UN's 17 Sustainable Development Goals that impact a billion people.

2. *Actualize:* Make it real for people. Be able to show the causes of the problem and the consequences to them that you are helping address.
   Doconomy wants to future proof life on earth. Their partnership with Ålandsbanken created the Åland Index that shows consumers the carbon footprint for each purchase they make, sensitizing them to the impact of their choices.

3. *Legitimize:* Demonstrate the problem by personalizing it to the stakeholder level by showing what it means to them.

Janice Lao showed airlines that the financial impact to them for going carbon neutral would not be harmful to their business. She developed the mathematical and economic model that the aviation industry uses for its carbon-neutral growth strategy.

4. *Utilize:* Show that you can generate or have created solutions that help solve the problem.
Divergent 3D's DAPS™ technology has built the first production hypercar based on AI-driven digital manufacturing that reatomizes materials, completely reinventing a 100-year-old highly inefficient, wasteful, polluting process.

5. *Expertize:* Use evidence to establish and/or associate your company as a credible authority/innovator.
Ravi Kumar of Infosys is creating thousands of jobs by building a new model for educating people and companies in the new world of work. The worlds of work, education, and skills development are more interdependent than ever, yet still too dependent on yesterday's thinking. Infosys is investing in new education models to prepare people and organizations for the world of tomorrow.

6. *Summarize:* Describe it succinctly and clearly to persuade others.
Change starts at the top. Helle Bank Jørgensen understood that meaningful business change needs a Board of Directors that are fully informed about sustainability, but most aren't. She started Competent Boards to address this need and has since partnered with academic institutions and industry partners to give Boards the understanding and fluency about sustainability issues.

## SO WHAT?

It's tempting to jump into solution mode when we're presented with a problem. We all do it. But while it might feel good, or even productive, problem-solving mode may lead to making the problem worse, or certainly taking you further away from a helpful solution. Why? Because we miss the bigger picture and fail to pay deeper attention to the underlying causes in our rush to diagnose and resolve. Even though we feel like we're applying our best experience and wisdom, and problem-solving gives us a sense of contribution, problem-solving mode blinds us to the creative ideas that more thoughtful exploration allows. I have written this book to give you broader context for how to prepare your company for transformation into a force for good. I didn't start off by saying "here's the solution." Firstly, because I don't have the solution, not even in this chapter on solutions. Sure, I could say that the answer to the climate crisis is to stop all fossil fuels–related activities. But that would create more problems than it solves. Secondly, those underlying causes are critical to tease out, much like a doctor who doesn't just treat the symptoms but focuses first on your health habits. Jumping to solutions short-circuits a more robust set of interrelated actions that, when examined further, can not only help solve the problem now but also greatly reduce the chances of it returning in the future.

Developing solutions that are sustainable means they have the following characteristics:

- An aspiration that guides decisions and *creates positive distinction* for your company.

- *Improved economic, political, and social outcomes* arising from their focus on fixing systemic environmental issues.

- Strengthened, not diminished, *stakeholder and partner ecosystems* because of their emphasis on cooperative work.

- Financial value as measured by how it *improves all stakeholders.*

- *More adaptable and responsive to changing conditions due to the new agile practices your company has implemented toward becoming a force for good.*


## END OF SECTION 3

This section focused on four value mobilization dimensions: stakeholder cultivation; stimulating engagement; enriching environments; and developing solutions. In sum, focusing more deeply on these four areas will help you answer the following questions

1. Which stakeholders do you need?

2. How will we build engagement with stakeholders?

3. What impact will we have on the environment?

4. How can our solutions be a role model for other companies?

Value Meaning, Value Measure and Value Mobilization have provided the logic, evidence and frameworks for transforming your business. The hard work is in reshaping your company around a force for good narrative that specifically tackles one or more of today's massive challenges as an integral part of your business strategy. This requires *Radical Business* practices, not business-as-usual approaches. All of the people featured in this book have deep experience in relentlessly pushing for transformative change, not just for their organizations, but on behalf of a healthier society and planet. They are not alone as they will be joined by you.

I encourage you to contact me and describe your efforts to transform your business. The more we share and learn from each other, the closer we'll be to meaningfully and measurably improving the world.

## NOTES

1. Adams, A. (1775). Massachusetts historical society. *Adams Family Papers*. Retrieved from https://www.masshist.org/digitaladams/archive/doc?id=L17 751127aa.
2. Based on 2021 author Interviews with Kevin Czinger.
3. Kronthal-Sacco, R., & Whelan, T. (2021). Sustainable market share index. Center for Sustainable Business. New York University Stern. Retrieved from https://www.stern.nyu.edu/experience-stern/about/departments-centers-initia-tives/centers-of-research/center-sustainable-business/research/research-initiatives/csb-sustainable-market-share-index.
4. See footnote 3, p. 2.
5. See footnote 3, p. 11.
6. See footnote 3, p. 33.
7. Edelman Intelligence. (2020). Trust barometer special report: Brand trust in 2020. Retrieved from https://www.edelman.com/research/brand-trust-2020.
8. Multiple sources: (1) Skånetrafiken website. (2021). Our mission-sustainable travel. Retrieved from https://www-skanetrafiken-se.translate.goog/om-oss/miljo/?_x_tr_sl=sv&_x_tr_tl=en&_x_tr_hl=en&_x_tr_pto=ajax,sc,elem; (2) Breschi, R., Freundt, T., Oreback, M., & Volhart, K. (2017). The expanding role of design in creating an end-to-end customer experience. McKinsey. Retrieved from https://www.mckinsey.com/business-functions/

operations/our-insights/the-expanding-role-of-design-in-creating-an-end-to-end-customer-experience.

9. Kowitt, B. (2021). PepsiCo is betting big on regenerative agriculture. *Fortune.* Retrieved from https://fortune.com/2021/04/20/pepsico-sustainability-regenerative-agriculture/.

10. Egan, M. (2021) To save the planet, tide wants you to quit using warm water for laundry. CBS Boston. Retrieved from https://boston.cbslocal.com/2021/03/18/tide-laundry-cold-warm-water-environment/.

11. Anthony, S. D., Trotter, A., & Schwartz, E. I. (2019). The top 20 business transformations of the last decade. *Harvard Business Review.* Retrieved from https://hbr.org/2019/09/the-top-20-business-transformations-of-the-last-decade.

# INDEX